DANGEROUS DAYS
IN THE
ROMAN EMPIRE

*A history of the terrors and the torments,
the dirt, diseases and deaths
suffered by our ancestors*

Terry Deary

PHOENIX

A PHOENIX PAPERBACK

First published in Great Britain in 2013
by Weidenfeld & Nicolson
This paperback edition published in 2014
by Phoenix,
an imprint of Orion Books Ltd,
5 Upper Saint Martin's Lane
London, WC2H 9EA

An Hachette UK Company

1 3 5 7 9 10 8 6 4 2

A CIP catalogue record for this book
is available from the British Library.

ISBN 978-1-7802-2635-4

Printed and bound by CPI (Group) Ltd, Croydon CR0 4YY

The Orion Publishing Group's policy is to use papers that
are natural, renewable and recyclable products and made
from wood grown in sustainable forests. The logging and
manufacturing processes are expected to conform to the
environmental regulations of the country of origin.

DANGEROUS DAYS
IN THE
ROMAN EMPIRE

CONTENTS

Introduction 1

Poison 7

Revolt 58

Disaster 75

Persecution 91

Instability 112

Insurrection 120

Calm 134

Cataclysm 147

Stability 159

Life 175

Shame 184

Turmoil 196

Misfits 203

Crisis 208

Nemeses 219

Decline 230

Fall 238

Epilogue 251

Index 257

For Billy Deary
(1906–1965)
Sine qua non

INTRODUCTION

The world has been full of dangerous people living through dangerous times. It's not always the dangerous people to blame ...

> 'The world is a dangerous place to live; not because of the people who are evil, but because of the people who don't do anything about it.'
>
> *Albert Einstein (1879–1955), German-born physicist*

Einstein may have had the Roman people in mind when he said that.

— THE VICTIM —

> 'Murder breathed her bloody steam'
>
> *Lord Byron (1788–1824), English poet,*
> *on looking around the ruins of the Coliseum*

The story of Vibia Perpetua and her friends is not a pretty one. She was one of the victims of Roman persecution.

Yes, *Roman* ... the citizens who had the effrontery to

call the rest of the world 'barbarian'.

Perpetua, a well-off North African woman, declared herself a Christian around AD 203. Her husband refused to be associated with a Christian so he abandoned her with her baby. It was a wise move.

The Roman emperor, Septimius Severus, had decreed that Christians must renounce their faith and burn a pinch of incense to the emperor as god. Perpetua refused. She and her slave Felictas were condemned to die in an arena along with two other Christians.

Her father begged Perpetua to reconsider – she was bringing so much disgrace on him. 'Don't get eaten alive. It'll show your old Dad up something rotten,' was the message.*

The four Christians were led to the arena where the crowds waited in feverish anticipation of a bloodbath. They got one.

Perpetua went along with 'shining face and calm step' – an enthusiastic martyr. Roman governor Hilarianus jeered at them. The Christians retaliated by telling him: 'You may judge us, but God will judge you and this city.' The words 'red rag' and 'bull' spring to mind … quite appropriately as it happens.

The furious crowd insisted the martyrs be whipped to prolong the agony of the occasion. The Christians were happy because they would be suffering the same way that Jesus had.

The women were forced to dress in the robes of the priestesses of Ceres, a pagan goddess. Oddly that enraged Perpetua more than anything and she struggled so hard

---

* Fathers everywhere will identify with the problem of children who show them up.

they gave up trying to dress her. Perpetua then began to sing a psalm.

For the young women, Hilarianus had prepared a mad, horned cow. So they were stripped naked and brought out into the arena. Even the crowd was horrified when they saw that, so the women were dressed in tunics.

First the cow tossed Perpetua and she fell on her back. Then sitting up she pulled down the tunic that was ripped along the side so that it covered her thighs. Next she asked for a pin to fasten her untidy hair: for it was not right that a martyr should die with her hair in disorder. If you were facing a wild cow would your last request be, 'Pass the hair gel'?

The report goes on to say that Perpetua 'seemed in a trance'. She asked 'When are we to be tossed?' and had to be shown the marks on her own body to convince her she'd already been through round one.

A second attack left her dying and she was thrown into a corner where it was customary for gladiators to cut the throats of the victims to make quite sure they were dead. But the Romans weren't happy with that in her case. They demanded that she be dragged to the centre of the arena so they could have a better view.

The young gladiator charged with the job was a bit nervous ... all those people watching gave him a touch of stage fright. He missed Perpetua's throat and stuck the knife into her neck. Perpetua cried out in pain, took the blade and guided it to her throat.* At last her ordeal was over.

---

* This sounds unlikely. Remember the report was written by someone trying to glorify Perpetua as a martyr. Just because someone 'said' something happened doesn't mean it 'did' happen.

— THE SPECTATORS —

> 'The only thing necessary for the triumph of evil is for good men to do nothing.'
>
> *Edmund Burke (1729–97), Irish statesman and author*

The civilized Romans had had their pleasure. Throughout history there have been blood-soaked cultures. The Aztecs ripped out beating hearts, for example. But they wanted to appease their demanding gods.

Even the Victorian British enjoyed a good public hanging. But they felt they were watching justice being executed.* They would argue the death set a moral example.

The French Revolution wanted rid of the aristos but used Dr Guillotin's chopping machine to make the deaths painless. The French turned out in their thousands to watch the spectacle but it didn't really qualify as a blood sport.

The Romans, on the other hand, built 50,000-seat arenas to watch the slaughter of humans. Not many were like Perpetua and went willingly to their deaths. Most went in terror. The Romans devised new and ingenious ways to prolong the suffering and extend their 'pleasure'. Killing humans was a spectator sport. And they called the rest of the world 'barbarians'.†

But of course the Romans wrote a lot of the history books and emphasized the glory that was Rome. To balance the

---

* No pun intended … or if it was it's not a very good one.

† The Romans borrowed a Greek word as a blanket term to describe their enemies: barbarians. (Because to Greek ears all foreign languages sounded like the bleating of sheep – 'baa-baa'.) But the Romans were just as much the black sheep of the world as their enemies.

books maybe we should look at exactly what it was like to live in the dangerous days of the Roman Empire. And exactly what it was like to die there.

Perpetua was confused after the first attack. What happened to her body? Dr Peter Fox MB, ChB, FRCGP, DrCOG* can tell us.

DANGEROUS DAYS DEATH I

ANIMAL ATTACK

The Mechanism of injury from a cow/bull tossing would be:

1. blunt injury to body – hit by heavy object
2. penetrating injury to body (if it has horns or kicked, breaking skin)

Shock clinically is about the effects of the body to compensate after circulatory blood loss, an overwhelming infection, heart attack or severe allergic reactions. As opposed to just being 'shocked' by your first bank statement after Christmas.

In this case Ms Perpetua probably has internal bleeding from the blunt trauma, as well as possible external blood loss from penetrating injuries. This would result in a drop in her blood pressure, less blood to brain, becoming drowsy and confused.

---

* Between you and me I thought Dr Peter made that last one up, but I checked and it means 'Diploma of the Royal College of Obstetrics and Gynaecology'. Now we know.

But NOT the loss of memory of events. For this I would expect her to have a head injury, either from being hit by the large bovine or from being tossed in the air and landing on her head (neither good). This would give her concussion, which would more likely explain the loss of memory of the recent events, the trance like state etc.

Under NICE guidelines she would go to hospital at this point, to undergo a period of observation and probably a brain scan as well. But in her situation then, even if brain scans had been available, the intention was not to treat her. Roman triage advice would be to avoid the bovine for as long as possible, take some paracetamol for the pains (if available) and give the crowd a good show!

Dr Peter Fox

POISON

'History is a pack of lies about events that never happened told by people who weren't there.'

George Santayana (1863–1952), Spanish philosopher and writer

The Romans once had kings. They were 'elected' kings, their role was more that of high priest, and generally they did a good job in helping raise Rome from a little city state to being an expanding menace to the whole region.

Lucius Tarquinius Superbus was the seventh king – unlucky seven (a.k.a. Tarquin the Arrogant … there's a clue in the name to the troubles ahead). He and his wife Tullia were so ruthless the Romans showed them the door and decided to run themselves as a Republic.＊

After 500 Republican years, their most powerful leader, Julius Caesar, was murdered on the dangerous ides of March, 44 BC. The main reason was that Caesar had been dropping strong hints he'd like to be king.† But that's another story for another day.

＊ Tullia's father, the king, was murdered. The 'grieving' daughter found his body in the street and drove her chariot over him.

† When I say 'they' murdered Caesar of course you know 'they' were about 60 of the top Romans. Like *Murder on the Orient Express* they all wanted to have a stab at it. Caesar ended with 23 stab wounds while the assassins managed to stab one another quite a few times too. Messy.

7

> 'Infamy! Infamy! They've all got it in-for-me!'
> *Kenneth Williams (1926–88) as Julius Caesar in* Carry on Cleo

Curiously the death of Caesar led to the death of the Roman Republic. The common people were outraged that their hero was murdered by a bunch of assassinating aristocrats. A Republic was as flawed a system as the old monarchy. Let's have a new dictator. Who? Caesar's friend Mark Antony? A bit unreliable. So who better than Caesar's grand-nephew and heir, Octavian.

Did you know ... Mark Antony

Mark Antony was beset by scandal. He attended a meeting in the forum and vomited because of a hangover. Tasteless. But was he really depraved?

Gossip spread of a wild Roman party at which a senior officer stripped naked, painted himself blue and mimed swimming on the floor wearing a fish tail. He was role playing the sea god. The gossips didn't specify where he stuck the fish tail.

Depraved? Or a typical Saturday night out in Manchester?

— AUGUSTUS (63 BC–AD 14) —

How do you get to rule the world?

First make friends with your biggest rival ... until you are ready to smash him. Octavian made friends with dead Caesar's ally, Mark Antony, and shared the Roman Empire with him. When Mark Antony started his scandalous affair with Cleopatra, Queen of Egypt, and neglected his duties, Octavian went to war and defeated him.

How did Octavian get the Romans to support him? If you have imperial ambitions then you need to remember the Chinese military strategist, Sun Bin's, factor for certain victory:

> 'The one who gets uniform support from his soldiers will win.'
>
> *Sun Bin (died 316 BC), Chinese military strategist*

How to be an emperor

- **Play dirty.** Octavian got word that Mark Antony had left his will in the keeping of the Vestal Virgins in the temple. Octavian seized the will and read it to the Senate. Antony's will said he left Caesar's legacy to Caesarion – the son of Caesar and Cleopatra. The Romans were outraged to think their inheritance was going to the Egyptians. They backed Octavian against Antony. Would you have read your opponent's private correspondence in public? Yes, if you want to rule the world. As China's other great strategist, Sun Tzu, said, 'All is fair in love and war.'

- **Delegate.** Octavian was no great general but he surrounded himself with competent generals – in this case Agrippa. You don't have to be the best at everything if you can hire the best. And Octavian had a peculiar (or convenient) habit of falling violently ill when danger threatened. At the sea battle of Actium, 31 BC, Octavian's admiral Agrippa out-manoeuvred

Antony's big ships.* Antony and Cleopatra ran away and died rather than face capture.

- **Be Wealthy**. The big bonus of defeating Antony and Cleopatra was that he pocketed the wealth of Egypt and took over his enemy's army. Octavian now had around 60 legions and scattered the veterans around the Empire to colonize it ... regardless of what the natives in the provinces wanted.

- **Be ruthless**. When Octavian defeated Brutus he had his head sent to Rome. To commemorate the first anniversary of Caesar's murder he had 300 nobles executed. Octavian had been Julius Caesar's adopted son. Caesarion had been Caesar's biological son with Cleopatra. Octavian didn't need that sort of competition any more than Richard III needed the Princes in the Tower. Octavian had 17-year-old Caesarion executed in Alexandria, following the advice of his teacher, Arius Didymus, who said 'Too many Caesars is not good'. A deadly variation on the 'too many cooks' advice.

Deadly shots

We think of broadsides as an invention from the era of Spanish galleons. But the Roman navies had catapults firing stone balls that could (and did) decapitate enemy sailors.

---

* This was a victory of the little ships against the unwieldy larger vessels in stormy seas. That would be echoed 1,600 years later when Drake and Frobisher famously defeated the Spanish Armada. The similarity ends there – there were no reports of Agrippa stopping for a game of bowls.

The Romans loved success and Octavian was the embodiment of their 'god' who had been Julius Caesar. The power of the people had made Octavian an emperor and he took the name 'Augustus'.

The people that hated kings had an emperor. A lot of Romans would live to regret it – a lot would die regretting it.

The Vestal Virgins

Who were these women who were so careless with wills?

1   They were the priestesses of Vesta – goddess of the hearth – who defended the city.

2   Their duty was to tend the sacred fire and make sure it never went out. There were six of them at any one time with a dozen novices in training.

3   The novices joined from the age of six and took a vow of celibacy for thirty years.

4   A Vestal Virgin who let the fire go out would be whipped.

5   Marrying a retired Vestal not only brought you luck but a very nice state pension too.

6   Any Roman could go to the temple and get a light for their domestic fire.*

7   A condemned person who saw a Vestal on his/her way to the execution would be automatically pardoned.

8   Vestal Virgins were daughters of the city – Roman men were sons of the city. So to have sex with a vestal was incest as well as treason. The punishment for a violated Vestal was to be buried alive in a cave. To add to your torment you'd be left with a little food and water. Nasty.

---

* Very handy since matches hadn't been invented … nor had the practice of rubbing two boy scouts together.

9 The unlucky man who was caught seducing a Vestal Virgin would be whipped to death.
10 The coming of Christianity led to the disbanding of the Vestals and the extinguishing of the flame in AD 394. Did Rome fall as a result? Rome fell within 20 years. Draw your own conclusions.

The good ...

■ Augustus improved Rome's infrastructure with aqueducts to bring in fresh water and the mighty sewer the Cloaca Maxima ... so mighty it even had its own goddess of sewers, Cloacina. Admiral Agrippa's greatest boat trip was to sail through the sewers to check that they were clean. From time to time, the sewers did get blocked and the forum was flooded with sewage. The posh had to hitch up their togas and paddle through poo. The outlet was into the Tiber and fish fed on the waste; they were then caught and eaten by the Romans. Tasty.

■ Augustus also pleased the poor (or 'appeased' the poor if you prefer) with generous doles of bread and shows – gladiator combats, athletics, sports and theatre. This pacifying of the mob came to be known as 'bread and circuses'. It's as if your government started giving away free televisions and chips. The down side is those circuses became the most cruel and violent 'games' in history.

The bad ...

■ Augustus named his step-son successor – making a top job hereditary is not the Republican thing to do.* The best men no longer got the highest job. Instead it went to men who were temperamentally unsuited to rule over picnic arrangements in a sandwich shop. Augustus's other mistake was to live too long.† His preferred successors dropped off their perches before he did. His eventual successor, Tiberius, was a soldier not a politician. If you were being kind you'd call Tiberius 'misunderstood'.

■ In 18 BC Augustus set out to clean up the Roman morals ... and went in for an early form of genetic engineering, encouraging the upper classes to breed. Three children got a man preferment in public office – refusal to marry had you debarred from your inheritance. Adultery was punished harshly. When his grand daughter Julia had a baby to someone other than her husband, Augustus saw to it that the baby was killed. His own great-grandson.

---

* Unless your name is George Bush, of course.
† As opposed to several emperors whose hold on life made a mayfly look like Methuselah.

Emperor spotting

Augustus was 5 foot 7 inches (1.7 metres) tall but wore stacked heels to appear taller. Suetonius wrote …

'His teeth were small, few and decayed, his hair yellowish and rather curly. His eyebrows met above the Roman nose and his eyes were clear and bright. His complexion was between dark and fair. He had seven birthmarks on his chest and stomach in the pattern of the Great Bear constellation. He dressed untidily and favoured a broad-brimmed hat against glare of the sun.'

He softened the hairs on his legs by singeing them with red-hot walnut shells.

And the mad …

- Augustus was a bad loser. Three Roman legions were wiped out in Germany thanks to the incompetent leadership of Varus – a relative by marriage. For months the emperor refused to wash or shave and wandered the palace banging his head against pillars while chanting, 'Varus, bring me back my legions.'*

- Augustus was capable of irrational behaviour which could be defined as 'mad'. For example he divorced his second wife for nagging him … what sort of man would do that? Augustus wore an amulet of seal skin in the belief it protected him against his biggest fear – lightning. A slave was struck while carrying Augustus in a litter.† There is a report that a Roman official

---

* I wonder if he banged his head in time to the chanting.
† This must have unbalanced the remaining carriers. Three wheels on my wagon, is the image that springs to mind.

approached Augustus with writing tablets hidden under his toga. The emperor was convinced it was a sword, had the man taken away and tortured. Then he personally tore the man's eyes out with his bare hands before sentencing him to death. The version Augustus gave was, 'The man attacked me!' He was sentenced to death, but this noble emperor spared his life and sent him into exile ... where he was never heard of again. A generous and forgiving emperor ... if you believe him.

BRIEF TIMELINE

27 BC   Octavius pronounced Imperator Caesar Augustus. The Republic is dead in all but name.

22 BC   An assassination plot by senators. It reminds 41-year-old Augustus he needs to plan his succession. He persuades faithful general Agrippa to marry his daughter, Julia, and become heir. Faithless failure Agrippa dies in 12 BC. So thoughtless.

9 BC   Augustus's step-son Drusus has been named heir but he falls off his horse and dies.* They are dropping like flies in a Flit factory.

6 BC   (probably) A baby born in Bethlehem called Jesus. Despite the efforts of the Roman client-king Herod to kill him the baby will survive 33 years and bring Rome a lot of headaches.

2 BC   Augustus's daughter – an orgy-loving lass – may have been part of a plot to overthrow her father. Her sons (Gaius and Lucius) were his heirs. Wicked woman packed off in exile.

---

* I could say, 'Heir today and gone tomorrow', but I won't.

AD 4   Grandson Gaius dies – murdered by stepmother, Livia, they say. Tiberius, the new heir, is recalled to Rome from a ten-year sulk on Rhodes. He needs to learn the business.

AD 9   Following the defeat in Germany Augustus becomes increasingly withdrawn from public life as Tiberius assumes more duties.

AD 14   As Augustus travels from Rome to Naples he falls ill.* He dies, aged 75, in the same room where his father had died. How weird is that?

As Augustus lay dying he turned to his friends and asked …

> 'Have I played my part in the farce of life well enough? Then send me from the stage with your applause.'

His friends probably agreed he was as farcical as they come and gave him a good clap. We do tend to say nice things to people when we know they are dying. Augustus, for all his little quirks (like murdering babies) was a top emperor. And, after reaching the top, it is usually downhill all the way.

— TIBERIUS (42 BC–AD 37) —

> 'People who make history know nothing about history. You can see that in the sort of history they make.'
> *Gilbert Keith Chesterton (1874–1936), British writer, critic*

---

* In the Middle Ages the Bourbon family coined the phrase 'See Naples and die'. Augustus would have complained that he *didn't* see Naples but died anyway.

The next bunch of emperors were probably the best models of the old adage created by Lord Acton. He wrote (with the wisdom of hindsight) …

> 'Power tends to corrupt, and absolute power corrupts absolutely. Great men are almost always bad men.'
>
> *Lord Acton (1834–1902), British historian*

Many people have heard the first part of that quote. Most haven't heard the interesting second part.* Lord Acton may have been thinking of the emperors of Rome when he wrote that – though he ought to have widened it to include 'men and women'. And maybe he ought to have included 'mad' as well as bad.

Because you'd struggle to find a more deranged class of human than the Roman emperors. Who were they and what did they do that was so bad/mad?

I'm glad you asked …

> 'Give the historians something to write about.'
>
> *Sextus Propertius (c. 45–15 BC), Roman poet*

Tiberius was 56 when he became emperor at a time when 50 was a ripe old age. But he lived to 77 so had a fair chance to leave his footprints on the sands of time.

It has been suggested that Tiberius was left at the front of the queue to succeed Augustus because his old mum, Livia, had ensured all the other heirs were bereft of life.

Tiberius was a notable warrior, but he was not cut out to

---

* Incidentally, if this Acton bloke was a 'Lord' then does that make him a great man? And if so is he calling himself a 'bad' man? You can't help but wonder.

be a politician. He was also the grumpiest old man since God sent Noah's Flood. He was a man who is quoted as saying …

> 'I don't care if they hate me so long as they respect me.'

He is the man who *should* have said …

> 'Start every day off with a smile and get it over with.'
> *W.C. Fields (1880–1946), American actor*

He was Augustus's step-son and married Augustus's step-daughter, Julia the Elder, to cement his hereditary rights. In effect he married his step-sister. Augustus had adopted him so he was the son of Augustus as well as his step-son. His step-father and father then became his father-in-law and his step-father-in-law. (Hope you are keeping up at the back there?)

Latin laugh

When Augustus died in AD 14 the legions in Germany revolted over poor pay and harsh conditions before Tiberius could get his feet under the imperial table. Germanicus was sent to quell the revolt, which he did by murdering some of the more brutal centurions … par for the course. The soldiers liked this and urged Germanicus to seize the throne for himself. He refused – the men insisted. He refused again … dramatically. He drew his sword, held it to his breast and said, 'I'd rather die – is that what you want?' A soldier was unimpressed by this drama-queen act; he drew his own weapon and said, 'Try my sword, sir, it's sharper.'

Tiberius tried to devolve power to the senate like in the good old days of the Republic. But the senators either didn't want it or were used to being told what to do. They didn't trust him or like him. He simply wasn't a people-person the way Augustus had been.

Disillusioned, Tiberius exiled himself from Rome (in AD 26) and left Rome in the hands of his ruthless general Sejanus. Sejanus took the elite Praetorian Guard from around the Empire and concentrated them in Rome. They were his private army and he began to eliminate his enemies – without keeping Tiberius fully informed of course.

When Sejanus finally overreached himself (in AD 31) Tiberius sent him a letter. Sejanus began to read it, smugly. Halfway through he realized he was reading his own death warrant. He was executed the same day.

Tiberius's revenge on everyone associated with Sejanus was pitiless. Historian Tacitus described it ...

'Tiberius ordered the death of all who were lying in prison. There lay, alone or in heaps, countless dead, of every age and sex, the great with the humble. Relatives and friends were not allowed close to them, to weep over them, or even to look at them too long. Spies were set to take note of the sorrow of each mourner and followed the rotting corpses, till they were dragged to the Tiber, where, floating or driven on the bank, no one dared to take them for cremation or even touch them.'*

Tacitus (AD 56–117), Roman historian

---

* Tacitus's tale is disputed. Some historians say Tiberius didn't execute THAT many plotters. So that's all right then ... unless you happened to be one of the ones he DID terminate.

So what was wrong with Tiberius? A competent general who helped expand and secure the Empire. But what was he like as a human being? Pliny the Elder called Tiberius 'the gloomiest of men'.

The good ...

- The Roman provinces did well under Tiberius. He knew a good governor when he saw one and let him get on with his job. That stopped fresh blood rising through the ranks, but at least there was a bit of stability in the provinces.

- Tiberius had a reputation for being tight-fisted yet when Rome hit an economic depression in 33 the emperor loaned 100 million sesterces to the treasury to stimulate money circulation. You could say he invented what we now call 'quantitative easing', 2,000 years ahead of his time.

- Tiberius left Rome to self-imposed exile on Capri but still attended to the business of government – he didn't 'abandon' Rome. The trouble is Tiberius was only informed of the business Sejanus chose to dispatch to Capri. And Sejanus had his own agenda. Why did Tiberius trust Sejanus, a man so twisted he could hide behind a corkscrew? Because in their early days Sejanus threw himself between a rockfall and the emperor. He saved Tiberius's life.

Emperor spotting

Tiberius was tall, heavy and strong. It was said he could punch a finger through an apple – or the skull of a boy. He walked with a slight stoop. His hair was auburn and hung below his collar. He was good-looking with large eyes and had a 'fresh' complexion. This was marred from time to time with pimples. So of all the emperors he's easiest to spot.

The bad ...

■ Tiberius was fond of little boys and liked to swim with slave boys in his baths. He called them minnows and the swimming involved sex games. He was also a voyeur and ordered threesomes to perform for him. The scandal-mongers suggested the emperor was into goats, donkeys and camels – some might ask, 'How do you hump a camel?'

> 'A farmhand was caught in the act with his cow. He said he had bad eyesight and thought it was his wife.'
> *Spike Milligan (1918–2002), Anglo-Irish comedian*

■ There was a punishment for any man caught going to the toilet while carrying a coin with the emperor's head on, a law against kissing, and a Grinch-like law to ban the giving of gifts at New Year. Disobedience to Tiberius was often punished by having legs broken.

And the mad ...

- Tiberius was notorious for his cruelty. He might make a man drink lots of wine ... then have the end of the victim's penis tied up. And talking about penises (well you started it) Tiberius passed a law which banned men over 60 from legally begetting a baby.

- There is a story that a poor fisherman on Capri caught a mullet and a crab and decided to give the huge mullet to the emperor as a gift. But Tiberius was in 'do-not-disturb' mode and was furious. He ordered that the smelly fisherman be scrubbed clean with the sandpaper scales of the fish. As the red-raw peasant staggered to the door he whined, 'Just as well I didn't bring the large crab I caught this morning.' Tiberius said, 'Go to this man's house and fetch the crab.'

BRIEF TIMELINE

AD 20 Over in Roman Syria the top Roman general (and heir to the throne) Germanicus is dead. He is the nephew of Emperor Tiberius and his popularity makes him a contender for the imperial throne. Germanicus's widow, Agrippina, thinks Emperor Tiberius has instigated the death. Poison is suspected. But the alleged poisoner commits suicide by slitting his own throat before giving evidence against Tiberius. Convenient.

AD 23 The commander of the Praetorian Guard (and the emperor's right-hand man) is Sejanus. He is becoming the most powerful man in Rome. But imperial heir Drusus doesn't like Sejanus – he punches Sejanus in the face. Mistake. Drusus is poisoned.*

AD 27 Tiberius sends himself into exile on Capri, and never returns.† Who steps in? Sejanus of course. Plots and poisons are working well.

AD 29 Agrippina is banished by Sejanus. She will starve herself to death in AD 33. Her sons, heirs to the throne, will die after accusations from Sejanus. Sejanus points the finger, Emperor Tiberius nods the head for the execution. Heir we go again.

AD 30 In a sideshow in Jerusalem a man called Jesus is charged with plotting to overthrow Rome. The Roman governor, Pontius Pilate, allows him to be executed on a cross. His martyr's death will come back to haunt Rome. Pilate error.

AD 31 Now Sejanus is overthrown. The Senate condemned him to death by strangling – his three unfortunate children will follow.‡ His body is

---

* This poisoning was so clever it wasn't suspected at the time. But Sejanus's wife turned informer in her suicide note eight years later. She said Drusus's cup-bearer and his doctor were to blame. They were tortured till they confessed. It seems Drusus's own wife Livilla had helped kill him. Livilla's punishment was to be starved to death by her mother. Becoming an undertaker seems to have been the surest road to riches in Rome.

† BUT ... it's said he tried to return twice. Once he sailed up the Tiber but turned back within sight of the city walls. The next time he travelled down the Appian Way. Seven Roman miles from the city he stopped to hand-feed his pet snake. He found it dead and half-eaten by ants. The ants, he believed, represented the masses and they would destroy him. He went back to Capri.

‡ His daughter Junila was, in theory, safe from execution because there was no precedent for executing a virgin. Her executioners sidestepped the problem by raping her ... with the strangulation rope already in place around her neck. A new precedent had been set.

thrown onto the Gemonian stairs, for the mob to tear
to pieces. Live by the sword, old boy ...

AD 37 Tiberius dies. Messily. His death was announced,
the crowds rejoiced ... only for servants to hear
the emperor call for food. Curses. Embarrassing.
Heir Caligula smothers him 'under a huge heap of
clothes'. Cheers.*

This 'keeping it in the family' certainly caused the problem of unsuitable men on the imperial throne. Tiberius
was great-uncle of Caligula, uncle of Claudius, and great-
great-uncle of Nero ... bringing the worst of both Acton's
worlds to bear on poor Rome. They were 'bad men' without being 'great men'. And they didn't come much badder
than Caligula ...

Did you know ... potted poet

Tiberius is said to have feasted for two whole days and
the night in between. When a poet called Tiberius 'fat'
the emperor had him thrown off a cliff to his death.
His enemies said that Tiberius liked wine ... but that he
liked blood even more.

Tiberius, like Augustus, was afraid of being struck by
lightning. Roman Historian Suetonius said ...

---

* It's classic pantomime isn't it? 'The emperor is dead!'
  'Oh no I'm not.'
  'Oh yes you are ... now.' Sadly this entertaining tale is probably as true
as Cinderella. Oh yes it is.

> 'Whenever the sky was stormy he was never seen without a laurel wreath, since they say the laurel is never struck by lightning.'
>
> *Suetonius (AD 69–c. 122), Roman historian*

— CALIGULA (AD 12–41) —

> 'Rome is a city of necks just waiting for me to chop.'
>
> *Emperor Caligula*

Caligula's father was Germanicus … the heir who had been poisoned. If Tiberius had prompted the poisoner then Caligula had his family's revenge by smothering Tiberius at the end … maybe. He later boasted that he had taken a dagger to the room where Tiberius slept, intent on murdering the emperor, but threw it to the floor unused.

Germanicus had taken his son on campaigns and had a little uniform made for him including hobnailed boots – *caligae*. The nick-name 'Caligula' or 'Little Boots' stuck like blood. And the new emperor would see plenty of that.

Little Boots appointed his uncle Claudius to be a consul. This was a man who'd been largely ignored in the persecutions because of his disabilities – his stammer, his lameness and his tendency to drool.

Caligula married Messalina, whose mother and father were both descended from the God, Augustus.

Everything in the garden looked rosy. Then Caligula fell seriously ill in AD 37. When he recovered he was a changed man – changed for the worse. The Roman historians don't go into detail – in fact information about Caligula is a little thin. But what has survived paints an ugly picture and is almost certainly not an accurate portrait – a bit like a Picasso painting.*

By AD 39 the emperor began to quarrel with the senate. He had started his reign by abolishing the treason trials, now he reintroduced them. Some senators were put to death, others were humiliated by being made to serve Caligula or run alongside his chariot.

Did you know ...

Caligula is said to have enjoyed drinking pearls dissolved in vinegar and to have served his guests with loaves and meats made out of gold.

To entertain his guests Caligula had criminals beheaded in the dining room as they feasted (and some people still like a nice chop for dinner).

He then alienated the people with his cruelty. There was one 'games' event where criminals were set to be eaten by wild animals. The crowds flocked in but they soon ran out of criminals. Caligula ordered a whole section of the crowd to be thrown to the slaughter instead. His excuse was he was bored.

His fatal mistake was to make fun of a Praetorian centurion called Cassius Chaerea. Caligula had mocked the centurion's squeaky voice and called him effeminate. Cassius Chaerea probably owed his voice to a wound in the genitals while fighting for Caligula's father, Germanicus. Caligula jeered at the man calling him 'Venus' – slang for

---

* Perhaps in reading Caligula's crimes we should put 'allegedly' after every sentence.

a eunuch – or 'priapus' (an erection)

Cassius, with the support of many senators and some of the Praetorian Guard, murdered Caligula at the Palatine games in AD 41. The centurion stabbed Caligula, appropriately enough, in the genitals. Revenge can never have been so sweet. The Praetorians didn't all support the plot and Cassius was arrested. He was one of the few to be executed in the aftermath – killed with the same sword he'd used on Caligula. That was his last request.*

Fellow conspirators synchronized sundials and murdered the emperor's wife and daughter at the same time. The baby had its head smashed against a wall. Caligula's end was as farcical as it could be – stabbed 30 times. His guards attacked and killed a few of the assassins, but managed to kill perfectly innocent senators at the same time.

The Praetorian Guard then sought out stammering, drooling Claudius to take the throne. Claudius (legend says) was found hiding behind a curtain in the palace, quite convinced they had come to assassinate him too.

Did you know ... small print

Caligula invented 'small print'. He passed tax laws without telling anyone so taxpayers were ignorant of them and he could impose punitive fines. When there were protests the historian says, 'Caligula finally had a notice posted, in an awkward spot in tiny letters to make it hard to copy.'

Our financial institutions wouldn't try a stunt like that nowadays. Perish the thought.

---

* That's a bit different. Traditionally, condemned men ask for a last ciggie.

The good ...

■ Caligula was popular at first – the crowd acclaimed him as 'Our Baby' and 'Our Star'. After all, he was following a reign of terror; he was loved because he *wasn't* Tiberius. He also set out to make himself popular – he gave a bonus to the elite Praetorian Guard to buy their loyalty. (Ironic, as we have seen.) He handed more power to the senate and gave the people the games and shows of blood they craved like Dracula. (The animals were expensive to feed until the days of the games. No problem. They were fed with the flesh of criminals.) He banned sexual perverts from Rome and had to be restrained from having them drowned.*

■ Caligula introduced 'Freedom of Information' rules when he made public finances open for inspection. He helped people who lost property in Rome's many fires and promoted new freedmen to the ruling classes. His new aqueducts were a marvel and he built a temple, a theatre and a racetrack for the people – as well as extending the palace for himself.

Latin laugh

At a sacrifice ceremony Caligula was handed a hammer. It was his ceremonial role to stun the animal that was about to have its throat cut. Very humane. Caligula's little joke was to whack the priest over the head with the hammer instead.

---

* A bit rich coming from a man who (allegedly) bedded all three of his sisters. Maybe it's a case of emperor's rules being different to us mortals?

The bad ...

■ One of Caligula's first acts following his illness was to eliminate his cousin, Gemellus, a man he saw as a threat.* The emperor's cousin was followed by his father-in-law Marcus Junius Silanus and his brother-in-law Marcus Lepidus. Uncle Claudius was only spared because his disabilities made him funny to have around. Even Caligula's greatest supporter, Macro, was helped to commit suicide. Macro, the man who had probably helped Caligula finish off Tiberius. Macro, the man who turned a blind eye when Caligula had an affair with his wife Eunia. There's gratitude for you. Macro and Eunia committed suicide. Caligula could make his feasts more fun by having someone tortured as he ate. At one dinner he brought in a slave who had stolen a strip of silver from a couch; executioners lopped off the man's hands, tied them round his neck and took him for a tour of the tables, with a sign showing what he had done to deserve it. He made parents go along to watch their children being executed.

■ The emperor was generous with gifts to the public at the gladiatorial games he provided. Of course it wasn't his money and the treasury was soon empty. Never mind, by falsely accusing a few rich people he could have them fined or executed and seize their wealth. He had his sister Agrippina exiled then sold her jewels, furniture and

---

* Their granny, Antonia Minor, was said to have been furious and then suicidal. Caligula's detractors hint that the emperor may have had had Granny Antonia poisoned. Don't feel too sorry for her. This was the woman who was selected to punish her own daughter for her part in the Sejanus plot against Tiberius. Antonia Minor locked her daughter in her room to starve to death.

slaves to fill his empty treasure chests. It worked so well he started to auction the contents of his old palace. He introduced new money-making taxes; there was a tax on marriage and a tax on prostitution … a her-charge surcharge? He would auction the lives of gladiators at the shows: 'You want your favourite fighter to live? Then pay up.' Centurions who had won riches from plunder were forced to hand it over to the state.

Incitatus

Caligula's horse, Incitatus (Swift), is famous because Caligula was said to have made him a consul. Consuls were the main men in the Empire – Incitatus would be the mane man. The story is unlikely. But it is likely that Inci was one pampered pony. A report said, 'Caligula would send out soldiers the day before the Games to order the neighbourhood to be silent, so that his horse Incitatus was not disturbed by noise. This horse had a marble stall and ivory manger, blankets of royal purple and a gem-studded collar. He had his own house and furniture, and a full team of slaves.'

And the mad …

- Caligula had been told by a soothsayer that he had 'no more chance of becoming emperor than of riding a horse across the Bay of Baiae'. So in a fit of pique he had a floating bridge built across the bay using boats as pontoons. That's over three miles. He then rode Incitatus across the bay while wearing the breastplate of Alexander the Great – he had robbed Alex's grave to get it. No doubt it gave him great satisfaction to thumb his nose to the soothsayer. But those boats should have been carrying grain to feed the hungry Romans. When the supply was interrupted, there was a famine in Rome. All so Caligula could say 'Nurr, nurr' to a fortune-teller.

Spot that emperor

Caligula was tall with an unusually large and hairy body. His scalp was almost hairless. He was a bit touchy about that hairy body so saying the word 'goat' in front of him would probably get you executed. He had a pasty complexion and a scrawny neck, sunken eyes and temples.

■ Caligula decided he was a living god. He began dressing as gods from Roman mythology. Hercules, Mercury and Apollo we can understand. But Venus? A little odd? In public documents he had himself referred to as Jupiter and had the heads chipped off statues of gods to be replaced with heads in his own image. He forbade people to look at him directly, though this may have had something to do with being sensitive about his incipient baldness.* Among the many depravities he was accused of, he was said to enjoy watching his victims being tortured. Imaginative punishments included covering the victim with honey and feeding them to a swarm of wasps …

---

* A Roman historian said, 'And whenever Caligula came across handsome individuals with fine heads of hair, he had the backs of their heads closely shaved to imitate his own baldness.'

... and the not-so-mad (maybe)

There is a story that Caligula marched to the north coast of Gaul to prepare for an invasion of Britain. When he reached the shore he ordered his men to collect seashells. Mad?

Or something lost in translation. 'Musculi' means seashells but it also meant military siege equipment. Was Caligula ordering his men to gather up the siege engines in preparation for a return to Rome where he feared there were plots against himself?

BRIEF TIMELINE

AD 37 Tiberius dies and the senate quickly disinherits one heir Gemellus in favour of the other, Caligula. Caligula then adopts Gemellus. Cousinly love. Nine months later he will have Gemellus executed. Cousinly caution.

AD 38 In just a year Caligula has managed to squander 2.7 billion sesterces that Tiberius had accumulated.*

AD 39 Caligula is said to have made his sister Drusilla pregnant and been so impatient to see the resulting baby he had it ripped from her womb. (What is true was that she died in childbirth.) He raises her to the status of a god. Drusilla's husband plots against Caligula but is executed and his bones scattered.

AD 39 Caligula thwarts a plot by German governor

---

* It was reported: 'He twice distributed three gold pieces each to the populace.' That's the way the money goes ...

Gaetulicus, then attempts a failed campaign against the Chatti tribe who, unlike the emperor, are not all talk.

AD 40 Caligula plans an invasion of Britain but then appears to get cold feet. His expansion to the west is more successful, thanks to some cheating – he invites Ptolemy of Mauretania to Rome. When Ptolemy arrives he is executed.*

AD 40 Messalina marries her second cousin, Consul Claudius. He is 48, she is 14.

AD 41 The Praetorian Guard were not appeased by that cash bonus from Caligula. Their plot to kill him wins support from the long-suffering senators, who draw the line at being obliged to worship him as a god.

AD 43 The Roman army finally gets around to invading Britain. It's a long struggle, but they will get there.

– CLAUDIUS (AD 10–54) –

'Moderation is a fatal thing … nothing succeeds like excess.'

Oscar Wilde (1854–1900), Irish writer and poet

---

* There are dozens of examples in history of leaders inviting rivals to friendly feasts and then having them killed. If you have an enemy who starts to act friendly, remember: when something seems too good to be true then it probably is. In Caligula's case this could have been a genuine offer. There is a story that the emperor saw Ptolemy's fine purple cloak and was jealous – he had him executed for spite, not politics. The ensuing Mauritanian revolt spilled gallons of blood.

If you want history to treat you kindly then get a good spin doctor to tell your story ... or hope there's a novel and television series made about your life that treats you sympathetically. Claudius achieved the latter when Robert Graves wrote *I Claudius* and *Claudius the God* (published in 1934 and 1935). He's regarded with a sentimental fondness; 'He wasn't all that bad.'*

He didn't feel comfortable with the ruling classes, the senators, so he tended to give freedmen the top jobs based on their ability ... not who their father was. On the down side there were a few chancers who took advantage of this opportunity, but generally Rome was ruled efficiently.

Claudius built bridges with the army. (No, not literally. Don't be silly. You know what I mean.) They planned the invasion of Britain in AD 43 and succeeded where even the great Caesar had failed. Claudius joined them ... after the army made it safe to do so, naturally. The only hiccup was what we'd call today a lack of an 'exit strategy'. Strange how that recurs throughout the ages. Maybe our war leaders should be reading this book?

> 'Those who cannot remember the past are condemned to repeat it.'
>
> *George Santayana*

Claudius was proving a competent leader. But by the end of the 40s he was starting to live down to Lord Acton's prescription and become 'a bad man'. In AD 48 the emperor had his third wife, Messalina, executed and married his niece, Agrippina.

---

* This is rather like saying 'Jack the Ripper killed only five or six women – far fewer than, say, the Yorkshire Ripper. So old Jack wasn't *that* bad!'

Agrippina was an ambitious woman whose prime ambition was to get her son Nero on the throne. He was only second in line. So Agrippina had Claudius's son (Britannicus) barred from being heir till he came of age at 14. All she had to do was make sure Claudius died before Britannicus reached manhood. That would be February AD 55.

There was no way the poor old emperor was ever going to reach that date. He wouldn't even make New Year. Late in AD 54 Claudius died.

Spot that emperor

Difficult to miss. Claudius has a tic, a speech impediment, a club foot, a mouth that is open and dribbling. His knees are weak, his head shakes. His nose runs when he is excited. Claudius's voice 'belonged to no land animal, and his hands were weak as well'. His laugh is uncontrollable.

BUT ... Claudius came to power and said he had exaggerated his infirmities so he'd look a harmless fool, no threat to anyone. No one feels threatened by a clown ... unless you are coulrophobic, of course.

The good ...

- Claudius was a competent politician; not as direct as someone like Guy Fawkes perhaps, but luckier. During his reign the Empire conquered Judaea, Thrace, Pamphylia, Lycia and Noricum. Fine, unless you are Judaean, Thracian, Pamphylian, Lycian or ... an inhabitant of Noricum. He also invaded Britain. Claudius might argue the Brits asked for it.

■   Claudius was a shrewd lawmaker. Slaves had been treated like a horse or a dog – If they fell sick they were taken to the temple of Aesculapius* and left to live or die. Claudius said that if they lived then they would be set free. And masters who had sick slaves 'put down' would be charged with murder. Some of his other laws are a little harder to empathize with in the 21st century. For example he passed a law encouraging people to break wind in public (in the belief that it was healthier than trying to politely hold it in).

The bad …

■   By the late 40s Claudius's private life began to get in the way of his public duties. He was estranged from his wife Messalina and took a slave girl as a lover … who in turn took lovers of her own. Messalina was reported to have enjoyed sex. She went to a brothel where she engaged in a competition to see who could 'cater for'† the most lovers in one night. Messalina won. When Messalina entered into a 'marriage' with one of her lovers she had pushed her luck too far. She had to go.

> 'Heaven has no rage like love to hatred turned, Nor hell a fury like a woman scorned.'
>
> *William Congreve (1670–1729), playwright and poet*

---

* Aesculapius had been a famous Greek doctor. Some of his cures actually worked. Others were a little more legendary lies. They say he cured a girl's water-on-the-brain by cutting her head off, draining it and sewing it back on. Don't try this at home.

† I do hope you appreciate that euphemism. Insert your own verb if you wish. I couldn't possibly do it for you.

In AD 48 Messalina was executed. Her fury was self-destructive in the end.

Fact file ... the execution of Messalina

In AD 41 Silanus was a Roman governor in Spain. He was recalled to Rome to marry Claudius's mother-in-law. But Claudius's wife, Messalina, fancied him for herself. When he turned her down she turned nasty and accused Silanus of plotting to kill Claudius. Their 'evidence'? She had seen the assassination attempt in her dreams. Silanus was executed.*

But be sure her sins did find her out. She plotted against hubby Claudius and, when he heard of it, he ordered her execution. She refused to take her own life so a centurion decapitated her.

When confirmation of Messalina's death reached Claudius at a banquet he said, 'More wine, please.' That's cool.

There is even a story that Claudius was so disenchanted by his experiences with Messalina he turned to his Praetorian Guard and said, 'If I ever marry again, please kill me.' He did. They didn't.

Claudius's freedmen advised a quick remarriage and recommended his niece, Agrippina. A British conductor once said,

---

* Manipulative Messalina persuaded Claudius to execute a lot of people she disliked. Sometimes she took more direct action. She sent a killer to strangle the future emperor Nero in his sleep. The attempt failed but the message is clear – you don't mess with Messalina.

> 'Try everything once except Morris dancing and
> incest.'
>
> *Sir Thomas Beecham (1879–1961), British conductor*

That only left Morris dancing for Claudius then.* It was
a fatal error. *Literally* fatal. Agrippina and her son Nero
used their power to poison Claudius and put Nero on the
throne.

And the mad ...

■   Claudius has a reputation as a benevolent ruler –
     encouraging the moribund senate to be more active
     in sharing the rule. But he was quite ruthless when it
     came to eliminating opposition. He had 35 senators
     and 300 equestrians executed as well as his niece Julia
     (sentenced to be starved to death), his father-in-law
     and (allegedly) his son-in-law, Gaius Pompey.†

■   It's said that Claudius liked to be present at the tor-
     ture of his enemies. He also like to watch men being
     executed by being flogged to death.‡

---

* Or did it count as incest? Claudius had the law changed to say marrying
your niece wasn't incestuous. It's wonderful what you can get away with
when you are a Roman emperor.
† Gaius Pompey may have been married to Claudius's daughter, Claudia,
but he was a naughty boy. He was stabbed to death in bed with his latest
boyfriend. He was a potential rival to Claudius, so Claudius has been
suspected of ordering the hack in the sack.
‡ He didn't, however, flog dead horses. That was the custom of British
supermarkets in February 2013.

BRIEF TIMELINE

AD 41 No sooner has Caligula been assassinated than Claudius is chatting to the Praetorian Guard about filling the boots of Little Boots. Did he know something about the plot to kill his nephew?

AD 42 Verica, king of the Atribates tribe in the south of England, is ousted by Caratacus. He runs whingeing to Claudius to reinstate him.

AD 43 Augustus had said the Roman Empire was big enough. Claudius decided it wasn't and set about adding to the territory by annexing places like Pamphylia and Lycia. Anywhere ending in 'a' seemed to be at risk.

AD 43 Claudius invades Britannia and captures the British capital Colchester.* It's rich in mines and slaves so it'll be a nice little earner. Claudius follows the advance invaders with reinforcements including elephants. He stays 16 days, which is not enough to start building Roman Roads ... or trunk roads.

AD 48 Empress Messalina gets the chop. No one ever deserves to be beheaded. But Messalina invited it.

AD 50 Brit King Caratacus is captured – he was betrayed by crafty Queen Cartimandua in the north of England – and taken to Rome for execution ... but is spared. He will live a comfy life as the guest of the Empire.

---

* Julius Caesar captured Gaul with the memorable war cry, 'I came, I saw, I conquered.' There is no evidence that Claudius captured Colchester and declared, 'The only way is Essex.'

AD 53   Nero marries step-sister Octavia. When it comes to inheriting the imperial throne there's nothing like keeping it in the family.

AD 54   Claudius dies. The finger of suspicion points to wife Agrippina and step-son Nero. If she hasn't personally poisoned Claudius then finger says she has a hand in it.

The end

There are several versions of the death of Claudius. Orson Welles put it cynically ...

> 'To give an accurate description of what never happened is the proper occupation of the historian.'
> *Orson Welles (1915–85), American actor, director, writer*

Most historians agree he was poisoned (though Roman historian Seneca said he died of natural causes). Most also agree his wife Agrippina and step-son Nero arranged it.

Claudius died at a feast after eating poisoned mushrooms. Roman historian Suetonius said ...

> 'Even if Nero wasn't directly responsible for the death of Claudius he was privy to it and openly admitted that. Afterwards he used to speak in praise of mushrooms as "The food of the gods".'

So who administered it?

- His food taster? A usual suspect. The eunuch Halotus kept his food-tasting job when Nero assumed the throne – surely Nero would have had him eliminated as an accomplice or as a witness to the assassination?

- Wife Agrippina? There had been a lot of domestics in the months leading up to Claudius's death. He complained about his misfortune in marrying four foul women. (Not a life-prolonging tactic for any married man.) Some claim she shared a plate of mushrooms with her husband, knowing which single mushroom was poisoned. (That could almost be an Agatha Christie plot.) Agrippina may have obtained the poison from the professional poisoner Locusta. Certainly the widow-making woman was richly rewarded by Nero in later years.*

- His doctor? It was claimed Claudius fell ill and the doctor suggested the emperor vomit to evacuate his stomach of the problem food. To facilitate the vomiting, Doctor Xenophon tickled the emperor's tonsils with a feather … but there was poison on the tip of the feather.

We'll never know for certain.†

---

* Agrippina had been desensitized by her life experiences. She'd had a traumatic childhood; her brothers were either killed or starved to death by order of the suspicious Emperor Tiberius. She had her first sexual experience at age 12 with her only surviving brother, Caligula. Does this explain her behaviour? Or excuse it? You decide.

† Maybe the story that Claudius was killed by a poisoned enema is true. It would NOT be the choice of exit strategy for many of us.

DANGEROUS DAYS DEATH II

POISON MUSHROOMS

So you've eaten some dodgy mushrooms, Death caps (Amanita phalloides). The bad news is you're going to die. The really bad news is its going to take up to a fortnight to happen. This mushroom is very poisonous with only 30g (one mushroom) needed to kill an adult. The toxins in the mushroom stop your cells reading from their DNA, the instruction book of your body, so the cells don't know what to do. They get confused, can't function properly and die.

For the first 10–16 hours after eating your meal of mushrooms you're fine. Then severe stomach cramps will double you up with pain, quickly followed by vomiting and profuse watery diarrhoea. For the two to three days these symptoms last your world will revolve around the 'latrinae'. After three days all your symptoms will settle down, and normal bowel service will be resumed. Unfortunately this apparent recovery is false. The toxins are continuing to destroy the cells in your liver and kidneys. Three days later the stomach pains, vomiting and diarrhoea start again, but this time you go yellow (jaundice). The kidneys also stop working with a consequent build-up of water in the body, resulting in your brain swelling, leading to confusion, fits and eventually a coma. Finally after about 14 days your heart stops and you die.

Dr Peter Fox

─ NERO (AD 37–68) ─

'Assassinations have never changed the history of
the world.'

*Benjamin Disraeli (1804–81), British Prime Minister and
novelist*

Ben Disraeli may have been a great PM and writer. But
this statement was not his finest hour.* Nero's ascent to
the throne had consequences that *would* change the world.
Forever. Sorry, Ben, you were just plain wrong.

Of the famous five first emperors, Rome saved the best
until last.

Nero started off well – didn't they all? He regarded
himself as a poet and a thespian. He built theatres where
he could perform and left the ruling to a team of competent professionals, handpicked by his mother Agrippina.
She in turn handed the reins to Nero's teacher, Seneca the
Younger (4 BC–AD 65). He was assisted by Sextus Afranius Burrus (AD 1–62), the commander of the Praetorian
Guard. Another seasoned pro.

The military exploits were left in the capable hands of
Domitius Corbulo (AD 7–67), who crushed a Parthian
revolt. So far so good.

Some of Nero's new laws were controversial. If a slave
committed a crime then all the slaves in that household
were guilty. In the resulting protests and revolts the army
executed 400 protestors. Harsh.

---

* See what I did there? 'Their finest hour' was a quote from Winston
Churchill, another British PM. I thought that was a neat juxtaposition.
You may feel it is just showing off. Oh well.

Then Nero fell out with Mum. Seneca excluded her from official business; it would be scandalous to allow her to sit in on negotiations with an Armenian envoy. Agrippina was not a happy lady. Nero disliked his step-sister-turned-wife, Octavia, and took up with an ex-slave, Claudia Acte. When Agrippina tried to intervene (like a 'Relate' counsellor) she was invited to sling her maternal hook.

Nero also took a male lover, Doryphoros, because, it was said, he looked like his mother. Nero may have been introduced to a taste for boy-favourites by Seneca, whose inclinations lay in the same direction.

Agrippina realized her mistake and started to back her step-son Britannicus for the throne. This was as maternally mindless as signing his death warrant. Britannicus died. 'Epileptic fit,' Nero claimed. Right.*

The more believable story is that professional poisoner Locusta gave a brew to the assassin. Britannicus had a 'taster' to check everything before he ate; but when Britannicus complained his wine was too hot, it was cooled with water. It was then the assassin struck – the poison was in the water.

Mum was banished and Nero could now show his true colours. Those colours would be mostly blood red. The emperor turned on his advisers. Praetorian Burrus? Accused of a coup plot. Seneca? Accused of embezzlement and having an affair with Agrippina.

Slave lover Acte was replaced by a new wife, the amber-haired Poppaea – or perhaps young Nero became her

---

* The famous poisoner Locusta was said to have mixed a murderous concoction. She 'tested' it on a slave. Animal Rights activists would be pleased no monkeys, rats or puppies were involved. The slave lived. Nero was furious and Locusta claimed her next potion would kill 'swifter than a viper'.

toyboy. She was said to be beautiful but immoral. Doryphoros objected to Poppaea. Doryphoros went from Nero to
Zero. The lad was poisoned in AD 62. What did he *expect*?

As Nero descended into megalomania his cruelties and
excesses became legendary. He wanted a large area of Rome
cleared so he could build a fabulous palace. His demands
were resisted until, as if by miracle, in AD 64 a devastating
fire cleared it for him.

Nero was blamed by the Romans but he turned it around
as neatly as any spin doctor, blaming the small Christian
community for the fire. To punish them, he had many
burned alive. The persecution of this tiny Jewish sect may
have been seen as having little significance at the time. But
of course it was the very persecution that strengthened the
resolve of the Christians. Everyone loves a martyr.

The Christians went on to dominate the world for centuries because Nero made them 'victims'. And Nero had
a hand in killing his predecessor. Still say 'Assassinations
have never changed the history of the world', Mr Disraeli?

There was an abortive plot to murder Nero during the
Circensian Games in AD 65, for which 13 people were
exiled and 19 executed. One victim was the great survivor
Seneca. He was ordered to commit suicide by opening his
veins in a hot bath. It was a slow and painful end for a man
who was probably innocent of the charges.

Revolts started in the provinces. The senate named Nero
a 'public enemy' and sentenced him to be flogged to death.
Without the help of his Praetorian commander, Tigellinus
(who was ill), Nero was friendless. His guards refused to
aid his escape.

Even his servants fled. When the soldiers came to arrest
him he stabbed himself in the neck. His secretary had to
finish off a botched job.

Famously Nero died with the words …

'What an artist dies with me.'*****

There have been better famous last words. Perhaps:

'I've had a wonderful evening … but this wasn't it.'
Groucho Marx (1890–1977), American comedian and film actor

The good …

■ Nero was inquisitive about science and inventions. He dismantled and reassembled a hydraulic organ to see how it worked. He initiated a lot of civil engineering projects and improvements to Rome. This was at a great cost to the treasury. He 'solved' the problem by devaluing the Roman currency. He even funded an expedition to discover the source of the Nile. (It failed because weed in the river blocked the explorers' progress.)

Spot that emperor

Nero was of average height, his hair light blond and set in rows of curls. His features were regular, his neck over-thick and his belly prominent. His legs were spindly and his face described as 'pretty rather than handsome'. He had a yellow beard which he shaved off to show his maturity. His enemies said he was spotty and rather smelly.

---

* Another suspect bit of reporting. If you had a sword in your neck you'd find it a bit hard to declaim your famous last words, wouldn't you?

■ Nero's Rome profited from having some good generals. One, Paulinus, crushed Boudica's revolt in Britain and tightened Rome's grip on Britannia. Another, Corbulo, brought the troublesome Parthians to heel. How would Nero ultimately reward this national hero, Corbulo, and one of the greatest generals Rome had known? In AD 67 Nero had him charged with treason and executed. What else? It proved a fatal error on Nero's part.

Fact file

Corbulo was a great believer in trenches to slow the progress of an enemy. He famously said:

'You defeat the enemy with a pickaxe.'

He didn't mean you hit them over the head with it. He wasn't technically 'executed' but ordered to kill himself. He literally fell on his own sword with a cry of 'Axios'. This is a cry made when a top clergyman is appointed. It means, 'He is worthy of it.' Maybe Corbulo meant, 'I am worthy of this.' Or in the vernacular, 'It serves me right.'

The bad ...

■ Some historians have tried to argue that Agrippina had an incestuous relationship with her son. Unreliable writer Suetonius put it crudely ...

'Whenever he rode in a litter with his mother he had incestuous relations with her, which were betrayed by the stains on his clothing.'

It may explain her anger when Nero took a mistress. Jealousy the green-eyed god.*

■ Nero, like Caligula, made trips in disguise to the seedy parts of the city, beating up passers-by. In AD 62 Burrus died and Seneca retired. One of Agrippina's ex-lovers, the callous playboy Gaius Ofonius Tigellinus (AD 10–69), became the new Praetorian commander. He shared in Nero's depravities.†

■ Soon Nero banished the innocent wife Octavia to the isle Pandateria. Her wrists were cut to make her death look like suicide.‡ For good measure she was suffocated in a hot vapour bath. Octavia's head was cut off and sent to Poppaea.

Nero wept and married a freedman (yes 'man'), Sporus, who was said to resemble Poppaea. He was dressed as an empress and given the name Sabina. Sweet. Ah, but Sporus/Sabina had to be castrated first to legitimize the marriage. Not so sweet then? Nero took Sporus/Sabina in his own litter through Rome, kissing him and cuddling him/her from time to time.

---

* 'Oedipus, Schmoedipus, what does it matter as long as a boy loves his mother?'

Jewish joke. 'Schmoedipus' being a word used as the title of one of Dennis Potter's (1935–94) plays.

† Tigellinus was a horse-dealer, promoted by Nero to command the Praetorian Guard. He is also a suspect in the Great Fire of Rome mystery. As the fire was dying down it sprang up afresh in another part of the city. Was Tigellinus the arsonist?

‡ In fact, wrist-slashing is a messy way to go. Writer Petronius was accused of treason against Nero. He did not wait for Nero's punishment, but chose suicide by repeatedly slitting and re-binding his wrists until he was drained of blood.

Nero then married another ex-slave, Pythagoras, and it was said that he acted as husband to Sporus and as wife to Pythagoras.

■ Nero fell for an actor called Paris ... but had him put to death, because his acting ability was greater than Nero's. Nero next fell for beautiful and wealthy Statilia Messalina. He had her fourth husband executed and made her his third wife in AD 66.

■ Nero became a luvvie. (He often wore an unbelted silk dressing-gown with slippers and a scarf. Very Noel Coward.) He ate leeks in the belief they sweetened his singing voice. But there was no escape for the audiences. When he recited his endless piece about the Trojan War the theatre doors were locked.* He was so good he won every contest he entered. The fact that he invariably bribed or threatened judges surely can't explain his success, can it? And he entered the Olympic Games to represent Rome in the ten-horse chariot race. His spectacular crash almost killed him and in another heat he dropped out. Of course he returned to Rome in triumph with the victory laurels. Bribery and threats again? Who says cheats never beats?

---

* Legend has it that women gave birth in the theatre rather than risk leaving. Others pretended to be dead in order to be carried out. To fall asleep was to risk imperial disgrace. Clapping the emperor was enforced by soldiers who prodded anyone who stopped too soon. The senate were embarrassed at the thought of their emperor performing like a common pop-singer, so they offered to award him the winner's laurel *without* the need for him to compete. He entered anyway. Amazingly he won.

Did you know ... fake Neros

History has been full of fakes. When Richard III's nephews 'disappeared' in the Tower of London a couple of imposters sprang up in the subsequent reign of Henry Tudor. And after Nero died there were several men claiming to be him. It seems for all his notoriety Nero remained a cult in parts of the Empire. Terentius Maximus (Great Terry?) appeared in the reign of Titus. He looked like Nero and – the proof of his claim? – he played the lyre just like Nero. Liar.

And the mad ...

- Nero decided his mum, Agrippina, had to go. He failed to have her poisoned – she was far too experienced a poisoner to fall for that one.

- Then he tried to arrange a collapsing ceiling over her bed. The plot was uncovered.

- Finally he persuaded his mother to take a boat trip across the Bay of Naples. Her boat was damaged so he insisted she take his specially prepared barge for the return journey. It glittered with jewels and had a silk canopy at the stern for her to sit, sheltered from the chill night breezes.

  They departed, best of friends ... he even kissed her breasts as she left. But his new boat had been sabotaged so that the stern, where Mum would be sitting, broke off and would leave her to drown. As Agatha Christie plots go, it had its advantages ... 'It was an accidental death, officer. Boating accidents happen all the time.'

The stern broke off but didn't sink. As the captain tried to force it under, his own sailors fought against him ... they couldn't swim! The tragedy was developing into a farce.

■ And, as an Agatha Christie plot, it was flawed. He hadn't accounted for the fact his old ma was a strong swimmer. Doh. She swam to land and the locals dragged her ashore.* She sent a message to Nero to say her ship had sunk ... but that she was safe. NOT the message Nero wanted.

■ Nero planted a knife on her freedman so he could claim she was plotting to assassinate him. 'Justifiable homicide, officer.' The emperor's advisers said it was Admiral Anicetus who promised Agrippina's death, so it was the admiral's responsibility to finish her off. Nero sent a troop of guards with the admiral and instructions to make it look like suicide.

■ All very plausible. But some historians just have to gild the lily and they make Agrippina's murder into a dramatic event. They *say* Agrippina saw them coming ...

---

* Agrippina's companion was even more clueless than Nero. Acerronia Polla went down with the sinking stern of the ship. She cried out that she was Agrippina so should be saved. Big mistake. The crew, who were part of the plot, believed her and bludgeoned her to death with their oars.

> 'The assassins closed in round her couch, and the captain of the boat first struck her head violently with a club. Then, as the centurion bared his sword for the fatal deed, uncovering her belly, she exclaimed, "Smite my womb," and with many wounds she was slain.'

The part of her body that had given birth to Nero. It may be 'historical record' but it is not a credible human action when someone approaches you waving a sword.

> 'History would be a wonderful thing – if it were only true.'
> *Leo Tolstoy (1828–1910), Russian novelist*

What *is* believable is that, after Agrippina's murder, the obsequious senators ingratiated themselves with Nero by sending him messages of congratulation. 'You have survived a wicked plot to murder you, oh great one ...'

And so evil thrives. One of the congratulatory messages came from Gaius Piso. He would crawl from the woodwork later with a fiendish plot. Watch this space ...

The other unlikely story is that Agrippina employed fortune-tellers long before Nero became emperor. They told her Nero would become emperor and that he would kill her. Her (alleged) reply was ...

> 'Let him kill me so long as he becomes emperor.'

If it were only true.

BRIEF TIMELINE

AD 54 Nero (age 17) and mum Agrippina murder their way to the top. He marries step-sister Octavia to cement his claim.

AD 55 Britannicus, son of Claudius, is step-brother to Nero and potential rival. He dies. How convenient.

AD 59 Agrippina dies. Nero suspected of having her murdered.

AD 61 Boudica the Brit leader revolts and spills a lot of Roman blood – both army and civilian.

AD 62 Nero marries Poppaea Sabina – a clean-living lady who bathed every day in milk.

AD 64 Much of Rome is destroyed in the Great Fire of Rome. Many Romans think Nero himself had it started to clear land for a new palace. Probably one crime he was NOT guilty of! Christians are blamed and persecuted. Paul of Tarsus, top Christian missionary, is executed.

AD 65 Pregnant Poppaea is kicked in the abdomen by angry Nero and she dies. She had criticized his gambling habit.*

AD 66 Nero has become a megalomaniac. Treason trials are resumed and taxes raised again to pay for his excessive lifestyle.

AD 67 Assassination plots shake Nero's confidence. Executing several top men won't stop his paranoia – or the plotters.

---

* It was said by one ancient historian that the wife of the traitor Piso was lined up to replace Poppaea. When she refused, Nero had her executed on a charge of attempted rebellion. Dead if you marry him, dead if you don't. Sometimes it's hard to be a woman ...

AD 68   Galba, the Roman governor of Spain, has himself
        declared Emperor.* He is gathering supporters (and
        armies) in the Provinces. Those provincial armies
        actually know how to fight – the Praetorian Guard
        have had an easier life and lose their bottle for battle.
        They declare for the rebels. Nero's goose is cooked
        and stuffed. When he hears his enemy at the gates –
        literally – he stabs himself.

The end

> 'Men do not care how nobly they live, but only how
> long, yet it is within the reach of every man to live
> nobly, but within no man's power to live long.'
>
> *Seneca (c. 4 BC–AD 65), Nero's guardian and teacher*

Nero was just 30 years old. He had not lived nobly and
it didn't look as if he was going to live much longer. His
glorious tour of the drama festivals had taken him away
from Rome. He returned to Rome when news of the discontent finally got through to him, by which time the city
was smouldering with resentment. For Nero had fiddled as
Rome burned.

Word reached Nero in his half-finished golden palace
that his loyal Praetorians had turned against him and were
supporting old Galba as the next emperor. In a fury, Nero

---

* Why shouldn't Galba declare himself emperor? After all, Nero had
just declared himself a 'living god'. You can declare yourself pretty much
anything you want to be, can't you? Of course Nero ordered Galba's
execution. Galba was expecting that – Nero was predictable if nothing
else – and Galba's soldiers simply intercepted the message.

tore up the message and overthrew the dinner table.

He ran the gamut of emotions from 'A' to 'B'. 'A' being Abject surrender, to 'B' being dressing in black and begging his people's forgiveness. He settled for 'E' for Egypt and decided to make a living as a wandering minstrel ... the winner of so many prizes could surely make a living from his massive talent? But for Nero it was the fat lady that was singing.

His back-up plan was to have the poisoner Locusta prepare a deadly draught for him. He stored it in a golden casket and slipped away to a villa in the Servilian Gardens to wait for a ship to Egypt.

The senate sentenced Nero to be executed. And still he waited for that ship. At midnight he rose to summon his guards. They had abandoned him. He went in search of servants but most of them had fled. Sinking ship and rats come to mind.

> 'An unpopular rule is never long maintained.'
>
> *Seneca*

When he returned to his bedroom the workers at the villa had stolen his rich bedclothes and the golden casket of poison. He called for his gladiator, Spiculus, to make a quick end. He didn't realize Spiculus had already been hacked down by the mob and his blood splashed over the fallen statue of Nero.

'Have I no friends or enemies left?' the soon-to-be-ex-emperor cried, making a run for the river. His remaining servants ran after him to stop him throwing himself into the Tiber. They decided to seek refuge in a country villa four miles away. Knowing it would mean a journey past the Praetorian barracks, Nero disguised himself in a faded cloak and a farmer's hat. He placed a handkerchief in front of his mouth … he could claim to be unwell if anyone asked.

As they set off through streets crammed with agitated Romans, an earth tremor hit the city. Lightning flashed. Apocalypse was on its way.* Nero rode to safety. But as Seneca said, 'No one can wear a mask for long.' Seneca was speaking in metaphors, meaning you can't hide your true nature for long. But in Nero's case it was literal.†

That fourth horseman, Death, was not going to be cheated. One of his corpses lay at the side of the road. Nero's horse shied at the scent and Nero used both hands to control it. The handkerchief fell away and a passing farmer recognized him.

A loyal soldier came to attention and called, 'Hail Caesar.' Oooops!

They reached the villa. Nero instructed his servants to dig him a grave in the garden. He could have quoted Seneca.

The fat lady's song was nearly over. A servant brought news that the senate had ordered him to be beaten to death with rods.

> 'Life, without the courage for death, is slavery.'
>
> *Seneca*

---

* Apocalypse is famously brought by four horsemen – Conquest, War, Famine and Death – riding on horses coloured white, red, black and pale. Oddly, Nero was accompanied by four horsemen. The colours of their horses are not recorded.

† As Nero had told Seneca to kill himself a couple of years before, it is hard to sympathize with him if he didn't have his old teacher's mask advice now.

Still Nero wasn't quite ready to die. He suggested his servants show him the way by killing themselves first. They declined. (Wouldn't you?) As a troop of soldiers were heard approaching, Nero asked a servant to help him thrust a dagger into his throat. 'Don't let them take my head,' he implored.

When the soldiers arrived Nero died in the centurion's arms. The servant Epaphroditus dissuaded the soldiers from decapitating him. The corpse was cremated.

Or was it?

For many years men claiming to be Nero appeared, with a lyre, in the east of the Empire. Had the servants done a switch with a Nero lookalike while the great artist escaped? The Romans took no chances and executed every Nero pretender.

REVOLT

— ROMAN REBELS I —
ARMINIUS (18 BC–AD 21) AND THE
CHERUSCI

'Remember that all through history the way of truth
and love has always won. There have been tyrants
and murderers, and for a time they seem invincible
but in the end, they always fall – think of it, ALWAYS.'

Mahatma Gandhi (1869–1948), Indian nationalist

(assassinated for standing up to the tyrants)

Not everyone loved the Romans. The Romans under
Augustus had the idea that the Empire could go on
expanding till it took over the world … and it would last
for all time. (The Third Reich under Hitler had similar
delusions but lasted a far shorter time.)

Many of the people in the conquered provinces stom-
ached the rule from Rome. Others found charismatic
leaders who would fight back and inflict painful defeats on
the Roman ego. A dangerous game that did not enhance
the rebels' life-expectancy.

In the case of Emperor Augustus the problem was not
treachery. It was stupidity and incompetence.

NEPOTISM, n. appointing your grandmother to power for the good of the party.

Ambrose Bierce (1842–1914), US satirist,
author of The Devil's Dictionary

Nepotism: keeping it in the family. It didn't work for the emperors because it was the family they had to fear most.

Fighting for Rome: Publius Quinctilius Varus (46 BC–AD 9)

Relative by marriage of Emperor Augustus. Augustus placed Varus in charge of the Roman legions occupying Germany.

Varus had a handful of weaknesses:

Arrogance. The Roman army had been triumphant under Augustus so, Varus reasoned, it was invincible. Of course the truth is it was unbeaten under great military commanders. Varus was NOT a great military commander.

Cruelty. When he governed in the Middle East he crushed a revolt in Judaea. He occupied Jerusalem and crucified 2,000 Jews. The Jews fought back by boycotting Roman pottery. Not quite so painful a retaliation, some might say.

Gullibility. The German tribes of the Rhine said they liked being ruled by the Romans. Varus believed them. In fact they were merely laying their plots like dragon eggs, waiting for them to mature then hatch.

Fighting for the rebels: Arminius (17 BC–AD 21)

Leader of the Cherusci tribe. The Cherusci were divided by the Roman occupation. Some factions supported the Romans.

Arminius a.k.a 'Herman the German' employed the arts of war as well as Sun Bin.

> 'The one who knows the art of war will win.'
>
> *Sun Bin*

Where did Arminius study 'the art of war'? From the crème de la crème. The Romans themselves.

He trained with them, rose to the rank of 'equestrian', then returned home to use that knowledge against his teachers.*

Even the Romans admired him. The writer Tacitus said …

> Arminius was without doubt Germania's liberator. He didn't challenge the Romans as an emerging nation, but at the peak of its empire; in battles, with varying success, he was undefeated in the war.†

---

* He has since gone on to become a symbol of German nationalism. 'Herman' was a popular name in Germany, though it suffered a little, post WW2, thanks to Mr and Mrs Goering naming their child Hermann. You don't see so many Adolfs around either, though it is a popular pet name for local traffic wardens.

† Which is not true. The Romans launched punitive raids into Germany, twice beating Arminius: in the Battle of the Weser River then at the Wall of the Angrivarii. Historians, eh? Can you believe them?

The revolt

Hold out baits to entice the enemy. Feign disorder, and crush him.

> *And ...*
> The one who is good at analysing and utilizing terrain will win.
>
> *Sun Bin*

● Arminius wanted to fight the Roman occupiers on his own terms and to choose the battleground. He went to Varus and told him, 'There is a rebellion in the north. The Chatti are planning to attack your Roman forts. We need to crush them before they link up with the Marsi and the Bructeri. You need to send your three legions to suppress it before it spreads.'

When Varus asked for a guide, Arminius was happy to help.*

Before they left, Arminius's father-in-law, Segestes, arrived to warn Varus it was all a trick. Varus didn't believe him and had him thrown out.

● A massive thunderstorm lashed the convoy as Arminius led the Romans deep into the Teutoburg Forest. Arminius's neighbouring tribes had 20,000 men hidden in the dense forest.

● The Romans like to march side by side, but those paths meant they had to walk one behind another. They like to march straight, but in Teutoburg they just made a

---

* A satnav may have done the job if it had been invented. Sadly for Varus, he had to rely on the locals ... which is about as reliable as a satnav, come to think of it.

ragged line, miles long. And the paths twist and fork, climb over rocky ridges and drop into boggy swamps. If you don't know the way you can go in circles for days. And they did.

- When they reached the deepest, darkest part of the forest Arminius dashed off and abandoned Varus.* The paths were muddy and the Roman wagons were bogged down.

- The Romans stuck. The German rebels struck.

- The Romans couldn't get into battle formation and had no experience of this sort of fighting. The Roman bows were too wet to fire and their shields were too soaked and heavy to carry.

- They managed to make a camp in the forest at night, but they were trapped. When they tried to break out, the tribes were waiting in the trees. The Romans were slaughtered.

- The camp followers included women and children: all were killed. There were tales of Romans being sacrificed to the German gods. They were cooked in pots and their bones used for ceremonies. Some captured Romans were placed inside wicker cages and burned alive.

- A Roman legion numbered between 4,000 and 6,000 men. Varus had three legions in Germany, the 17th, 18th and 19th legions. Along with their families and servants, there would have been around 20,000 men,

---

* Can't help hearing echoes of *Babes in the Wood* or *Hansel and Gretel* and wicked stepmothers here. Very Germanic.

women and children who went into the Teutoburg Forest.

● Very few came out. Most were killed in battle or made into slaves. The Romans never again used the numbers 17th, 18th and 19th for their legions – they were unlucky.

● Varus fell on his sword and killed himself.

The end

Six years later the Romans sent a new army to northern Germany. When they reached the forest they found heaps of white Roman bones and skulls nailed to trees. Their guts had been strung out over the tree branches. They buried the remains.

Arminius turned from Roman conqueror to fighting his neighbours. He seemed to enjoy war. But his end came away from the fields and forests of war. First his neighbours, the Chatti tribe, told the Romans they could have Arminius poisoned. The Romans were very sniffy about that offer, saying they preferred to avenge their defeats on the battlefield not the dining room. (This is a bit rich, given the number of Romans who popped their clogs after eating toxic teas.)

Arminius had sent the head of Varus to Marbod, the leader of the greatest German tribe, with the message, 'Join us in the fight against the Romans. See? We can win!' Marbod sent the head to Emperor Augustus in Rome to be buried. Marbod didn't join Herman ... instead he went to war against him.

Emperor Augustus was crazed with grief at the defeat.

Twelve years after the battle in Teutoburg Forest, in AD 21, Herman was murdered by his nephew, who felt he was becoming too powerful. Echoes of Julius Caesar there. As someone very clever said …

> 'Keep your friends close and your enemies closer.'
> *Misattributed to Sun-Tzu. In fact a quote from Michael Corleone in* The Godfather, Part II

Top man's nephew got the top job – just like Augustus and Varus.

And, just like Augustus, he discovered a terrible truth … your nephew is often your worst enemy.

— ROMAN REBELS II —
BOUDICA (DIED AD 61) AND THE ICENI

> 'If particular care and attention is not paid to the ladies, we are determined to foment a rebellion and will not hold ourselves bound by any laws in which we have no voice or representation.'
> *Abigail Adams (1744–1818), US First Lady, 1776*

> 'the Ancient Britons, though all well over military age, painted themselves true blue, or woad, and fought as heroically under their dashing queen, Woadicea.'
> *From* 1066 and all that, *W.C. Sellar and R.J. Yeatman*

In AD 59 Gaius Suetonius Paulinus became the new Roman governor of Britannia. Some tribes welcomed him, some were hostile, but it was the Druids who really annoyed him. He let these wild Welsh worshippers distract him so much he neglected the tribes in the east to attack the west. When the cat's away ...

Fighting for Rome: Gaius Suetonius Paulinus (born AD 1)

> 'Every great man nowadays has his disciples, and it is always Judas who writes the biography.'
>
> *Oscar Wilde*

Famed for being the first Roman to cross the Atlas Mountain range in North Africa, Paulinus led a whole legion across in AD 41. It took him ten days of marching to reach the snow capped summit. The thoughts of his frozen-footed-and-fingered fellow marchers is not recorded. They tracked down their Moorish enemies in their mountain strongholds and crushed them. Good practice for fighting the Britons in the Welsh mountains.* Paulinus ruled the place we now call southern England (roughly from the Wash to the Severn estuary) with his veterans. It was the druids of Anglesey that needed to be taught a lesson.

Paulinus reached the Menai Straits and crossed into Anglesey. The Welsh thought they'd be safe from the

---

* Highest Atlas mountain: 4,167 metres. Highest Snowdonia mountain: 1,085 metres. Makes the Romans climbing through Snowdon look like a stroll in the park ... well, a stroll in the park with Welsh warriors leaping out of the flowerbeds to ambush you and cut your throat.

Romans behind the watery barrier, but the Romans rode and swam across.

The Roman writer Tacitus described the scene when Paulinus invaded. And it made pretty gruesome reading ...

> 'On the far shore stood the forces of the enemy, a dense show of arms and men, with women dashing through the ranks like the furies; their dress was black, their hair dishevelled, and they carried torches in their hands. The Druids stood around the fighting men, pouring forth horrible curses, with their hands uplifted towards the heavens. They struck terror into the Roman soldiers by the strangeness of the sight; it was as if the Roman limbs were frozen, they could not move.'

Tacitus was a bit of a sycophant, so of course he made Paulinus sound like a hero.

> 'The brave Paulinus said they would not be scared by a rabble of women and madmen. The Romans attacked. They smote* all the Welsh and wrapped them in the flames the Welsh had lit. The Romans killed everyone who stood in their way, including the women and Druids who carried no weapons.'

The Romans tore down the sacred temples where the Druids had carried out their sacrifices. Tacitus said the

---

* 'Smote' is a really good Biblical word. It means 'battered' but sounds more exciting.

Romans found the trees dripping with human blood.[*] They then turned the tables on the enemy by drenching their sacrificial altars in Druid blood. The entrails of the victims fell to the woodland floor and were 'read' (like tea-leaves) as horoscopes.

Then Paulinus received word of an Iceni rebellion over in East Anglia. Time to wipe the stale Brit blood off his hands and head east to collect some fresh.

Fighting for the rebels: Boudica, queen of the Iceni

Boudica was not a woman you messed with. According to Roman historian Cassius Dio ...

> 'She was huge and terrifying with a harsh voice. A great mass of bright red hair fell to her knees: she wore a twisted necklace, and a tunic of many colours, over which was a thick cloak, fastened by a brooch. Now she grasped a spear, to strike fear into all who watched her.'

The Iceni were a revolting people. They had rebelled in AD 47 when the Roman visitors set about disarming their 'client' tribes. The pro-Roman king was killed and the Romans put in a new puppet, Prasutagus. His wife became queen. We don't know her birth name but she got the appendage

---

[*] Without modern forensic science they couldn't possibly know it was 'human' blood, the Roman defence lawyers will argue. The presence of disembowelled humans in the area is circumstantial evidence and can be disregarded. As I must repeat, milud, Tacitus was four years old at the time and wasn't there.

'Boudica' meaning 'Victorious.' (This is rather like Richard I of England being known as 'Lionheart' and the world forgetting he was ever called Richard.)

Mrs Prasutagus ... or Boudica ... took her place at the head of the tribe. She would have enjoyed the Roman lifestyle and had a responsibility to crush any further rebellion against Rome ... for the moment.

The rebellion

Then King Prasutagus of the Iceni died. Lots of people have done that, and we're not blaming him for it, but the king's big mistake was to write a will and leave his kingdom under the joint care of the Romans and his two daughters.

The Roman orator Cicero (106–43 BC) had explained that women have 'a weaker intellect' than men so are not fit to rule a hen house let alone their own house. He wasn't a feminist.

When her husband died, Boudica would have expected the emperor's financial agent, Catus Decianus, to comply with the dead king's will. Instead he robbed the Iceni tribe of its treasures and humiliated its nobles. When Boudica dared to protest, she was publicly flogged. Her princess daughters were raped in an act that was pure provocation. If you pull a tiger's tail, expect to be scratched ... or eaten.

Flogging was as much a public humiliation as a punishment. That didn't lessen the pain for the flogees, of course. It could lead to death ... whether that was the intention or not. How?

DANGEROUS DAYS DEATH III

FLOGGING

The Romans knew a thing or two about whipping a person to death. First they would strip you naked before tying you to a pillar, either being stretched out or bent over it. Not wanting to kill you straight away, they whip you from behind, so that your vital organs are protected and a fatal blow early on in the proceedings is less likely. To make things more interesting the whip or flagellum is not only made of several strands of leather but has sharp pieces of bone and lead added to the tips.

Two really big blokes, known as lictors, then wield the whips, taking alternate blows to your body from the shoulders all the way down to your feet. As they warm to the task, the combination of the thick leather and sharper additions cut through the skin. The pain is intense, blood starts to ooze from the wounds, the blows continue. Unremitting, they cut deeper through the subcutaneous tissues and into the muscles. The oozing becomes a steady stream of blood as deeper veins and arteries are cut. Your flesh comes off in long ribbons, exposing the ribs and bones beneath, and with each blow a mist of blood fills the air. All you can do is scream.

The good news is that eventually, by losing all this blood, you go into hypovolaemic shock. With less blood circulating, your brain becomes starved of oxygen, you become confused, then finally your heart stops and you die. Occasionally on a 'feeling kind and good' day they may stop whipping you before this all happens, but with no antibiotics, overwhelming infection will kill you two to three days later.

Boudica was forced to repay the Roman invaders money that was technically a loan, but which the Iceni believed was a gift. Prasutagus had taken the equivalent of today's pay-day loan to burnish his public image.* Now it was payback time. And Boudica had no money.

To the Romans, rape was an offence against a woman's guardian (hubby or dad) but not against her personally. Boudica and the Iceni took a different view. They rebelled.

They ensured their neighbours were complicit ... no point in attacking the alien invaders if the folk next door are going to stab you in the back.

● First they attacked Colchester – a town garrisoned by Roman veterans. The inhabitants had bad omens. Tacitus said ...

'Without any evident cause, the statue of Victory at Colchester fell and turned its back to the enemy, as though it was fleeing before them. Women agitated to frenzy foretold impending destruction. Ravings in a strange tongue were heard in their Senate-house. The theatre echoed with wailings, and in the estuary of the Thames there appeared an overthrown town; even the sea had taken on the appearance of blood. When the tide ebbed, there had been left the likenesses of human forms. These wonders were interpreted by the Britons as hopeful ... but by the defenders as alarming.'

---

* Nero liked to lend large sums to tribal leaders – the interest was a very nice earner for Rome. But it also put the tribe under an obligation to their Roman 'benefactors'. Sneaky politics.

- Catus Decianus sent less than 200 troops to help. Some help. As Colchester burned, Decianus fled to Gaul, which gives a whole new meaning to taking French leave.

- Boudica attacked Roman towns and historian Cassius Dio said she was especially cruel to women prisoners. Roman women were hung up, naked, had their breasts cut off and sewed to their mouths, so it looked as if they were eating them. Afterwards they were impaled, having a sharp wooden stake pushed through their bodies, and they were hoisted up for everyone to see.

- Tacitus said the Britons couldn't wait to cut throats, hang, and burn and crucify. The 9th legion marched to the relief of the town. Tough, experienced and professional. But they were ambushed and massacred. The cavalry (and their commander) fled on horseback and left the foot-soldiers to their fate. Thanks chaps.

- Having left Colchester a smoking ruin, Boudica's troops then marched on London. Paulinus wisely evacuated the city before it went up in flames. The Romans ran from St Albans before the arsonists arrived.

- The Londoners were left to the mercy of Boudica's rebels ... and mercy was a word that didn't feature in her vocabulary. Archaeological efforts have uncovered decapitated cockneys, men and women, from this period.

- London was a trading port at that time, not a Roman military settlement. Not every Briton hated the Romans. A lot of yuppies were rather taken with the

Roman lifestyle and Boudica didn't get a tidal wave of support from south of the Thames. Maybe torching the city was her way of making her point to the southern folk. Maybe she wanted to destroy the bridge across the Thames to protect her rear when she turned north to pursue Paulinus? Whatever her motive, the outcome was straightforward. London's burning.

● Paulinus headed for St Albans and decided, yet again, to abandon it to the rebels.* As he marched from Roman settlement to Roman settlement he was gathering troops all the time. Around 10,000.

● Boudica was gathering more. Around 230,000. Do the math.†

● It's said that around 70,000 Romans and their sympathizers died ... but again these are Roman estimates and they had their own reasons for inflating the figures.‡

The end

The Romans regrouped and started to fight on their own terms – in an open battle, somewhere on Watling Street. The outnumbered but heroic Romans (Roman version) faced the wild British barbarians.

---

* He could have quoted the Ancient Greek Demosthenes (384–322) who said: 'The man who runs away may fight again.'
† A truly dreadful phrase from our American cousins who massacre the language as efficiently as Boudica massacred Romans. I can only apologize for using the phrase in a moment of weakness.
‡ Like a fisherman and a tale of the one that got away. 'Yes, we lost, but you should have seen the scale of the problem. I wasn't fighting a tiddler, you know.'

Roman historian Tacitus (born AD 56) was clearly not at the battle in AD 61 but he claimed Boudica made a grand last speech. She insisted she wasn't a queen fighting for her lost wealth but a Briton fighting for the freedom of her people and that God was on their side.* She said ...

> 'Heaven is on the side of a righteous revenge; one legion which dared to fight has already perished; the rest are hiding or are thinking of running away. They can't resist even the war-cries of so many let alone our charge and our blows. We must win this battle or die. Let the men live as slaves if they want to. I won't.'*

And of course she didn't live as a slave.

Her army of (an alleged) quarter of a million faced the ten thousand Romans under Paulinus.

The Roman general's speech to the troops was more practical. According to Tacitus he said ...

> 'Ignore the noise made by these savages. There are more women than men in their ranks. They aren't soldiers – they're not even properly armed. We've beaten them before and, when they see our weapons and feel our spirit, they'll crack. Bring them down with your javelins and finish them off with your swords.'

---

* Guy Fawkes would claim the same thing a millennium and a half later. It didn't do him much good either. The difference is Boudica is now held up as a symbol of Brit Grit while Guy is abused as a treacherous murderer. But at least he didn't stitch Roman breasts to Roman mouths.

The Roman army dutifully obeyed. Paulinus chose a narrow battlefield (somewhere in the Midlands) so the Brits couldn't use their numerical advantage. The Romans used a wedge formation to drive the Britons back to where their own families and followers had formed a ring of supply wagons. The trapped tribes were slaughtered: 80,000 of them died to only 400 Romans. Result.

Boudica is then lost to history. Did she fall ill and die or did she take poison to avoid capture? Is she buried under Platform 8 at King's Cross Station (as some say)?*

Paulinus exacted revenge. His massacres probably killed more than Boudica had done. His diligence in killing off all opposition led to him being relieved of his command by Nero and recalled to Rome under a cloud. Thanks, Paulinus, let's reward you with a slapped wrist.

> 'Blow, blow, thou winter wind, Thou art not so unkind as man's ingratitude.'
>
> *William Shakespeare (1564–1616), English poet and*
> *playwright*

---

* Yes, people HAVE died on Platform 8 while waiting for a delayed train. But they usually passed away from old age. It is more difficult to ascertain whether any joined Boudica in a glass of poison while waiting for the last chariot to Norwich. There is absolutely no evidence for Boudica's burial there being true. It's just one of those stories we'd all love to be true ... like King Richard III being buried under a Leicester car park.

DISASTER

— THE GREAT FIRE —

I fell into a burning ring of fire,
I went down, down, down,
and the flames went higher,
and it burns, burns, burns,
The ring of fire.

'Ring of Fire' lyrics by June Carter and Merle
Kilgore (1963)

One spark of fire can change the history of the world. Forever. No one knows exactly where the spark that started the Great Fire of Rome fell. It was probably an accident … but arson has been suspected.

It is called 'The Great Fire of Rome' rather like 'The Great Fire of London'. The forgotten fact is it should be called 'one-of-the-great-fires-of-Rome'. It's only 'great' because of the consequences.

The key facts

1 A fire broke out in Rome on the night of 19 July 64. The emperor at the time was Nero. Tacitus (who was there at the time) said Nero was 35 miles away, playing his lyre.*

Historian Dio disagrees. He says Nero was on the roof of his palace on Palatine Hill in Rome. Since the Palatine Hill and its buildings were consumed by the fire, Nero would have had to play very fast then run even faster. Did Nero 'order' the fire? Again Dio chips in with the rumour …

> 'Nero secretly sent out men who pretended to be drunk or larking about and set fire to one or two buildings in different parts of the city. The Roman people were confused because they could see no start of the fire or any way to put an end to it.'
>
> *Cassius Dio*

Tacitus said it started in a single location – the Circus Maximus.

Another source is historian Suetonius, who went still further and said Nero lit the fires personally …

> 'Nero pretended to be disgusted by the dingy buildings and the narrow streets, Nero shamelessly set fire to the city. A group of ex-consuls caught Nero's servants with flaming torches entering their property but were too afraid to intervene.'

---

* Tacitus was nine years old at the time and couldn't vouch for Nero personally. Even if Nero's alibi was firm as Roman marble, there was nothing to prevent him from instigating the conflagration. The story of Nero playing the lyre was written 165 years after the fire by historian Dio.

Even if it seems unlikely Nero started the fires himself, the emperor could still have been the instigator.

Why would Nero want to set fire to his own city? In order to clear the way for a vast new palace. That is the legend.

2 The Circus Maximus was the world's largest wooden building ... ever. It was a stadium for drama, mime and song contests holding 200,000 people. But above all it was a chariot-racing track. Four teams, the reds, whites, blues and greens raced in chariots pulled by any number of horses from two to ten. It was dangerous and exciting. It was fiercely partisan with rival colours enjoying all the animosity and violence of today's football supporters.* The charioteers were the football idols of their age and made fortunes when they were successful.

3 Nero was a massive fan of the chariot races and a supporter of the green team. He wanted to be a charioteer himself but his advisers said it would be demeaning to ride around in public. He had a private track built and raced to his heart's content. But in July AD 64 Nero missed a three-day race meeting to head for the seaside. (Tacitus does not record if he took a bucket and spade.) It was rare for the emperor Nero to miss this sort of event. Did he have an ulterior motive for appearing to be out of town? An alibi for his absence from the scene of the crime? The crime of arson?

---

* Roman racing fans were like football supporters in tunics and sandals. Tunics at football matches are not a sight you see in many British football grounds – not even Arsenal – so maybe it's not the best metaphor ever devised. Sorry.

4 The day of the fire, 19 July, was one of the hottest days of the year. As Nero prepared himself for a singing contest, 35 miles away, the crowds flocked to the Circus Maximus. While Nero was singing* of the Wooden Horse and the part it played in the destruction of Troy, back in his capital the wooden-horse-arena was about to play a part in Rome's destruction. The Circus had arcades beneath the outer walls selling snacks to the supporters. You could buy bread and fish, pastries and sausages, roast thrushes on sticks and all manner of tasty treats and drinks. The proximity of so many hot-food braziers adjacent to a wooden arena would not have got past a deaf, dumb and blind Health & Safety officer. Rome didn't employ such an officer. 'Accident waiting to happen' is the phrase that springs to mind.

5 One of the cooking fires got out of control. Some say it was a sausage stall. Adjacent shops sold lamp oil. What arsonist could ask for a better accelerant? Flames leapt, dry wooden stands (and fat greasy sausages) fuelled an unstoppable blaze, fed oxygen from a northerly wind. The Circus became a fiery oval like a Hindenburg disaster. The moon shone down on a roaring, smoking shower of sparks.† Night-watch soldiers rang warning bells as the residents nearest the Circus fled. But a fireball on that northern wind could run faster than they.

---

* Not singing but singeing in fact.
† And as it was just two days off a full moon, some historians have argued it couldn't have been arson … no respectable fire-starter would wander the streets under the light of the silvery moon, would they? But if they were lurking in the shadows of the stadium what would they care if the moon was glowing green as a fluorescent cheese?

6 The tenement blocks were fodder for the blaze. The wooden shutters caught fire and flames swept upwards through the floors, causing the buildings to fold in on themselves, swallowing anything and anyone inside, blocking the narrow streets and barring escape for the survivors ... At first the night-watch ran with leather buckets to fight the fires. When that didn't work they'd have been ordered to pull down houses to create a fire-break. But how can anyone guard against sparks falling from the clouds? They must have soon realized the futility and fled to save their own homes.

> 'Men fighting the fires were told that their own homes were on fire. Before they reached those homes they'd be told they were already destroyed.'
>
> Cassius Dio

The fire spread south on the wind but seemed to erupt from everywhere.

> 'When a citizen turned to look at the flames behind them they discovered they were assailed by flames to the side of his face.'
>
> Tacitus

That was the terror that led to the rumour of multiple fires being started simultaneously by Nero's henchmen. Not henchmen, just random embers.

We can only imagine the terror, standing inside a ring of fire with every exit route blocked by walls of flame or fallen buildings, and the smell of burnt timber mingling with the scent of your own eyebrows smouldering.

Human horror brings out the best and the worst in

people. There were those shining saints who perished trying to rescue others. On the dark side of the street there were looters, there always are, the sheer thrill of being able to snatch something for nothing ... even if you don't need it.* We don't know if any Roman went to help a fallen fellow citizen then used the opportunity to rob him ... but it certainly happened in the London Riots of 2011.

And strangest of all, the pyromaniacs. Savages throwing burning torches into buildings that *weren't* yet alight. 'Recreational violence' as one reporter called it when it happened in 21st-century London.

> 'The past is a foreign country, they do things differently there.'
>
>   *L.P. Hartley (1895–1972), English novelist*

Oh no they don't, LP.

7 Nero had won his song contest. He shrugged when he heard about the fire on the morning of 20 July. Then a second message came to say the perverse wind had swung around to threaten his own palace in Rome. Orders sped back to Rome: 'Save Nero's property!' Nero sailed back to Rome to organize a relief effort, which he paid for from his

---

* The examples are endless. In the Blitz of WW2, as bombs fell and people hid in shelters, the looters entered the unguarded houses. Where were the police? Some of them were leading the looting. When Hurricane Katrina struck the US in 2005 you can understand the people who forced their way into shops for water and food. Even beer. But television sets? When your house is as flat as an IKEA flatpack? Where were the police? Some of them joined the looters.

own funds. He ordered a swathe of buildings to be demolished as a fire-break and the Gardens of Agrippina opened to the homeless multitude. Grain was delivered from Ostia and the price of bread reduced. An exemplary effort on Nero's part. So how did he feel when he began to hear the rumours that he was to blame? A little miffed? A touch angry? Or very afraid? And out of that fear arose the urge to blame someone. 'Blame anyone. Just don't blame me,' he must have moaned. That's when history gets as murky as the skies over Rome.

8 Six days and seven nights later the wind dropped and the fires finally died. The bodies that weren't reduced to ash began to rot. Nero ordered the removal of all the rubble along with the corpses.* Rome would be rebuilt. But even as the Circus Maximus was turning into the Circus Minimus, the blame game had started.

> 'A rumour had gone forth everywhere that, at the time the city was in flames, the emperor had appeared on a private stage in Antium singing about the destruction of Troy, comparing the Rome disaster to that of the ancient one. It seemed Nero wanted the glory of founding a new city and calling it by his own name.'†
>
> *Tacitus*

---

* An easy order to give. But it had to be executed by the slaves, the Praetorian soldiers and the night-watch. Not a job for the squeamish.

† The name being Neropolis. 'All roads lead to Neropolis' doesn't have a very euphonious ring to it. 'The glory that was Neronium' – sorry, doesn't work for me. 'Nero wasn't built in a day' and 'When in Nero do as Nero does' … They maybe have a surreal truth to them.

The rebuilding was to commence immediately ... and the provinces would make a huge contribution.* Nero would be the town planner and building regulations manager; wider streets, lower tenement blocks, colonnaded porches to serve as fire-fighting platforms. But 1,750 years before the Luddites roamed the mean streets of England there were reactionaries in Rome who complained. You can hear them supping on sour wine in the taverns and moaning (in Latin), 'The broad streets mean less shade and all that heat has to be unhealthy. When I were a lad ...' Still, Rome rose like a goldrush town.

Nothing could resurrect the scorched reputation of Nero.

> 'All the efforts and all the gifts from the emperor did not banish the troubling belief that the fire was the result of a command. Therefore, to rid himself of suspicion, Nero fastened the guilt on a class hated for their outrages.'
>
> *Tacitus*

9 In the wake of the fire, he made a new urban development plan. Houses were to be spaced out, built in brick, and faced by porticos on wide roads. Nero also built a new palace complex known as the Domus Aúrea in an area cleared by the fire. To find the necessary funds for the reconstruction, taxes were imposed on the provinces of the Empire.

---

* We can imagine that did not go down well. Your boss's house is gutted. 'Great. I never liked him.' But we're increasing your insurance premiums several hundred per cent to have it rebuilt, so he can live in a luxurious and grand new home. 'You what?'

10 So who did Nero blame? Legend has it that it was a little Jewish sect in the city called 'Christians'.

The script of Tacitus said famously …

> 'To get rid of the accusations, Nero fastened the guilt and inflicted the most exquisite tortures on a class hated for their abominations, called Christians. Mockery of every sort was added to their deaths. Covered with the skins of beasts, they were torn by dogs and perished, or were nailed to crosses, or were doomed to the flames and burnt, to serve as a nightly illumination, when daylight had expired.'
>
> *Tacitus*

Some historians have claimed Nero actually blamed an Egyptian cult – the devotees of Isis. Christian monks copied the Latin manuscripts and inserted 'Christians' instead of followers of Isis. That made the early Christians martyrs and heroes of the Church. Unlikely theory.

What is pretty certain is that the priests (of Isis or Christ) were arrested, tortured and 'confessed' that they started the fires.*

Their followers were imprisoned and as soon as an arena was available they were executed. The victims were wrapped in animal skins and packs of wild dogs were set loose to tear them apart.

Others were crucified. But the cruellest fate of all was reserved for the ones who were soaked in oil and raised

---

* If you were on a primitive rack, with the sinews of your arms and legs slowly tearing, you might confess to being responsible for the Fire of Rome … or the Great Fire of London, or the sinking of the *Titanic*. (Well *somebody* pushed that iceberg, and it's no use you trying to blame those poor polar bears.)

on poles and set alight to illuminate the emperor's gardens, which were opened to the public. Their screams were meant to be part of the entertainment. Yet this display of fire seems to have back-fired on Nero.

> 'Even for those criminals who deserved public punishment there arose feelings of compassion. These executions were not for the good of the public, as the emperor claimed.'
>
> *Tacitus*

Few Romans believed Nero was blameless where the Great Fire of Rome was concerned.

The game of consequences

> 'Is it so terrible a thing to die?'
>
> *Virgil (70–19 BC), Roman poet*
> *(quoted by a Roman officer as he deserted Nero in AD 68)*

After the Great Fire there was punishment for scapegoats. But the fire probably did lead to Nero's demise. It was time for the Piso plot.

✦   Gaius Piso had been the senator who'd hosted the party where Nero's mother had eaten her last supper. He had also been among the first to congratulate Nero on the close escape from assassination when Nero's mother was butchered. Yet Piso had plans to kill Nero and have himself elected emperor. The public discontent over Nero's alleged involvement with the fire gave him the confidence to proceed.

◆ He was supported by Flavius Scaevinus – a man with extensive properties in Rome. They were destroyed in the fire, he had no insurance and his creditors were pressing. Elevation in the Roman ranks would make him rich enough to solve his problems. He threw his hat into the ring with Piso.

How to get yourself executed ...

One of the Piso conspirators met a condemned man. He decided to cheer the man up by saying, 'Never mind, Nero won't be around much longer and the new emperor will set you free.'

The condemned prisoner reported this remark to the authorities. The conspirator was arrested and tortured and gave away the names of the plotters. He then took the condemned man's place.*

◆ If the plotting was sophisticated the actual murder attempt was stolen from a very bad pantomime script. Nero would attend the next chariot races. A muscular plotter called Lateranus would approach Nero and throw his guards off the scent by kneeling in supplication. (Are you picturing this?) He would then grab

---

* A woman called Epicharis knew about the plot. Her captain-lover complained Nero didn't favour him. She said that Nero would die soon. She thought he'd join the conspiracy. Far from it, he turned her in (the rat). She was tortured with branding irons and whips and crushed limbs, but unlike the man she refused to betray any names. Her gaolers carried her in a sedan chair to another round of torture because her legs were already broken. She strangled herself with her girdle, which she fastened to the chair. Tough lady.

Nero's legs and wrestle him to the floor. Bankrupt Flavius Scaevinus would have the honour of striking the first blow while the other plotters restrained Nero's guards.

◆   Brilliant? Or barmy? We'll never know because the plotters were betrayed and executed. Scaevinus's odd behaviour alerted his servant, Milichus, who shared his worries with his wife in bed. For a start Scaevinus didn't even like chariot racing. And for another the master had given him a sacred dagger to sharpen.*

◆   The servant's wife said he had to run to warn the emperor. If the plot were discovered, and Milichus kept quiet, he would suffer. Her arguments (or nagging) were persuasive. Milichus ran to Nero's palace and handed over the incriminating dagger. Scaevinus was arrested … and brazenly accused Milichus of lying.

◆   Then Mrs Milichus stuck in her oar again. She revealed that their master had held secret meetings at the house with an equestrian called Natalis and that the servants had been excluded. Unusual. Suspicious.

◆   Nero used classic police procedure to investigate. Inspector Morse would have been proud of him. 'What was the meeting about?' Nero asked Scaevinus. Then he had Natalis taken to a separate room, allowing no contact with Scaevinus. 'What was the meeting

---

* Top tip to wannabe assassins: Sharpen your knife. Scaevinus discovered his was rusty and handed it to a servant to clean. This is a bit of a giveaway. Either sharpen it yourself or stab the emperor with a rusty knife … he's not going to die of blood poisoning, is he?

about?' Inspector Nero asked. The stories didn't tally. Inspector Nero had his evidence.

✦ The Praetorian Guard just had to show the torture implements to Scaevinus and Natalis. They sang like canaries in a pear tree.

✦ The plotters were arrested and Inspector Nero used another surprisingly modern technique to root out the conspiracy – every arrested man was offered immunity from prosecution if he could name one other plotter. It worked.

✦ Piso opened the veins in his wrists and the Praetorians arrived in time to lop the head off his dead body.*

Death of a teacher

Nero's guardian and teacher, Seneca, was implicated (maybe wrongly) and ordered to commit suicide. The centurion who took the message refused to allow him to write his will. Seneca sighed and declared ...

> 'I leave you the noblest possession I have ... the example of my life.'
>
> *Seneca*

That is gobsmackingly hypocritical. Seneca said many wise things and notably failed to live up to them. He was

---

* Meanwhile the plotter Lateranus who was detailed to grab Nero by the knees was arrested by Tribune Proximus. Lateranus was relieved. He knew Proximus was a plotter. Lateranus was then 'relieved' of his head by the sword of Proximus. Dead men tell no tales. Proximus got away with murder. He later committed suicide.

a convicted adulterer and certainly a serial plotter. His words of wisdom included …

> 'It is not the man who has too little, but the man who craves more, that is poor.'
>
> *Seneca*

Yet he spent his life making sure he accumulated wealth like a snowball accumulates mass. He was a man who had started to believe his own press releases. Follow his 'example'? I think not.

Seneca's young wife begged the centurion to behead her, but Nero's orders were for her to live. Seneca urged her to join him … which seems rather selfish. He placed their arms together and with one stroke slashed both of their wrists, then left. His wife simply made a mess of blood on the floor. When Nero heard of her attempt he ordered, 'I forbid her to die.' Her wounds were bound and she recovered.

In another room Seneca dribbled on and lived on through the night. His doctor gave him hemlock to speed his end. He lived on.*

His doctor ordered hot baths to be prepared so the old man could suffocate in the steam. A drama queen to the end, Seneca dipped his fingers in the water and sprinkled it on his slaves. 'I offer this tribute to Jupiter.' Jupiter must not have been listening (or not grateful for a sprinkling of warm water) because Seneca refused to die.

So he was carried to a hotter bath to encourage the blood to flow. It worked at last and Nero's teacher finally slipped away and was chalked off.

---

* Seneca was a philosopher but also famous for writing tragedies. His own end was more Spamalot than Hamalet.

His head was removed by the centurion and sent to Rome as proof of his death.*

Painful purging

The Great Fire encouraged the plotters to intrigue. When they failed, heads rolled. Literally. One after another was beheaded.

The treacherous tribune Flavus was ordered to kneel by fellow tribune Niger. Flavus then rather tempted fate by telling Niger, 'I trust that your blow is firm, Niger.' No pressure, then, Niger.

What happened next? Nervous Niger botched it and took a couple of hacks before Flavus headed off to heaven.

And the Great Fire was followed by a plague in Rome, a devastating hurricane in Campania and a huge fire in Lugdunum. Romans began to mutter that this was divine retribution for Nero's crimes. Then came the Jewish revolt and that was when Nero started persecuting Jewish sects like the Christians.

He gave orders that all Jewish prisoners throughout the Empire should be executed. The Christian Saint Peter died (probably) in February AD 67. He was not a Roman citizen so his sentence would have been crucifixion. He requested the painful death of being crucified upside-down.

The apostle Saint Paul followed several months later. As a Roman citizen he had the honour of being beheaded. No one could have predicted that 250 years from these deaths

---

* Yes, I know, it would have been less trouble if the head had been removed in the first place. But suicide was regarded by the Romans as taking your fate in your own hands – dignified and heroic. Seneca would have argued, 'Execution is undignified.' But, Seneca mate, it is so much quicker.

the little Christian faith would become the official religion of Rome.

Did you know ... Nero's acting

Nero had 'Singing' introduced as a new event in the Greek Olympics ... and he won it of course. He then went on to the Isthmian Games in Corinth (winning the verse, song and charioteering prizes).* He also developed a taste for acting in Greek tragedy. As in Shakespeare's day there were no women allowed on stage. One of Nero's characters was a pregnant woman. In another he played a prisoner in chains. One of his German guards was so convinced his emperor was a prisoner he rushed on stage to set him free. What a trooper blooper.

---

* But not at the same time. Racing a chariot while singing 'Two wheels on my wagon' would have been entertaining but sadly it didn't happen.

PERSECUTION

— GREAT GODS AND CRUELTY TO CHRISTIANS —

> 'Piso's a Christian, he worships a fish;
> There'd be no kissing if he had his wish.'
>
> *W.H. Auden (1907–73), Anglo-American poet,*
> *from 'Roman Wall Blues'*

> 'Most history is a record of the triumphs, disasters, and follies of top people. The black hole in it is the way of life of mute, inglorious men and women who make no nuisance of themselves in the world.'
>
> *Philip Howard (1933—), author*

The Christians revered martyrs. Jesus had been crucified and from the very start they were persecuted. Just a year after Christ was crucified a follower called Stephen was stoned to death in Jerusalem. Their crimes were against Jewish orthodoxy.

Judas hanged himself, of course, but of the remaining eleven apostles only one (John) died of natural causes.

Once the Romans started picking on the Christians the Jewish persecutions paled into insignificance.

Rome is famous for its persecution of the Christians from Nero to Constantine – around 250 years. But it wasn't a conveyor belt of Christians to the lions. It was more like the Wars of the Roses in England ... generally remembered as years of continuous conflict, yet they weren't. There were only a dozen major Roses battles. Twelve days of fighting in 30 years of 'war'.

And in the 250 years of 'persecution' Christians lived most of their lives in peace and safety with only occasional purges in certain parts of the Empire.

———————

TEN THINGS YOU (PROBABLY) DIDN'T KNOW ABOUT THE CHRISTIAN MARTYRS

1   The Roman gods

'There is no place in our city that is not filled with a sense of the gods. There are as many days fixed for annual sacrifices as there are places where they can be performed.'

Livy (59 BC–AD 17), Roman historian

The Romans felt threatened by the Jewish–Christian idea of a single God. 'Come on,' they said, 'how can *one* God look after all the blessed things that need ... well ... blessing? Look at some of the things a single God could easily overlook ...'

- Door hinges – Cardea will look after them. We may need that priestess of pivots, and altar to an axis.

- Cupboards – the Penates are deities that will look after our storerooms and your sideboards, our closets and our cubbyholes. Of course in return they'd expect to be worshipped with shrines and offerings. At a family meal we may throw scraps of food on the fire as an offering.

- Mildew — Robigus is god of mildew (that mouldy fungus that grows in damp places), and agricultural diseases like 'wheat rust' (that well-known cereal killer). He's a nasty little beggar who has to be propitiated with offerings. He can give or take away the nasties from our farm.*

- Beer – Sabazius is god of barley and beer and generally any plants that are not a crop. (So he is a useful chap to encourage our flowers or weeds to grow.) His symbol is usually a snake.

- Boundaries – Terminus is not the god of bus stations but the god of boundary markers and will keep out trespassers. (No, you couldn't make it up.) On 23 February we need to sacrifice to Terminus. He is partial to the blood and bones of sacrificial victims, or a sprinkling of lamb's blood,† but will make do with honey or wine.

---

* The best sacrifice comprises the blood and entrails of an un-weaned puppy. Yes, quite disgusting. Please do NOT try this at home. What they did with the flesh of the puppy is not recorded, but we can guess.

† I say 'sprinkling' but the Romans would aim to drench their boundary stones with the blood of a lamb or pig. The most accessible form of pig's blood these days is black pudding. There is no record of anyone testing this to see if it protects your home against trespassers like (say) burglars.

● Goddess of other things – Furrina is a goddess, but by 100 BC no one could remember what she was goddess of. Some scholars think she may be the guardian of springs bubbling water or bubbling wine. Her festival is celebrated every 25 July, so champagne is called for on that day (or sparkling water if you must).*

The trouble is the Romans KNEW their god-system was right because poets like Virgil (70–19 BC) had written poems in which Jupiter declares ...

> 'I have given the Romans an empire without end.'
>
> *Jupiter, top god, quoted in* The Aeneid

So anyone who *didn't* subscribe to the Roman gods was a heretic, and heresy has been punished with death throughout time. The Christians were going to find it hard to survive in Imperial Rome.

2   The diviners and the charlatans

> 'How flattering to the pride of man to think that the stars in their courses watch over him, and show, by their movements, the joys or the sorrows that await him.'
>
> *Charles Mackay (1812–89), Scottish poet, journalist*

Divination is from a Latin word meaning 'to foresee' or

---

* You see a lot of bubbling water in a flushing toilet, of course. Maybe she should be revived as the goddess of toilets? Every flush a tribute to Furrina? Toilet rolls named after her? A whole commode cult and a sanitary sect for the poor, neglected and forgotten deity.

'inspired by god'. In other words, if you can read the signs from god then he'll tell you what is going to happen.

Rome was full of sign-readers – often astrologers who said the gods' messages were in the patterns of the stars. You don't need to read them for yourself, just go to an astrologer and they will read them for you ... usually in exchange for a payment.*

And to help your god make that a 'good' future you can buy lucky charms. Rome had lots of charm-sellers to has sle you in the streets. (But no charity fundraisers to pester you.)

Most of us have seen the sellers of lucky charms on our own streets and been tempted to point out the flaw in their sales pitch ...

SHABBY LADY: Want to buy some lucky heather?

SMART CYNIC: If it was that lucky you'd be living in luxury not wandering the streets.

SHABBY MAN: Can I sell you a lucky rabbit's foot?

SMART CYNIC: It didn't do much for the rabbit ... and it had four!

Now you may think this is modern wit but, sorry, the Romans were there first with their scepticism.

The cynic Ennius said ...

---

* Today you can read your stars in the newspaper and the astronomer's fee is part of what you pay for the paper. This is quite a bargain because the Romans didn't give you the sports results, the gossip, the latest bad news and the television times all thrown in for the price.

> 'I think nothing of the augurs, the entrail diviners, astrologers who hang around the circus, Isis-seers or interpreters of dreams. They are lazy, mad or ruled by want. They do not know the path to take for themselves, yet they show the way to others. They beg a coin from those to whom they promise riches. Let them deduct their fee from what they promise and give back the rest.'*
>
> *Quintus Ennius (239–169 BC), Roman writer*

Today's diviners read tea-leaves (tasseography) or Tarot cards. The Romans had a typically tasteless alternative (as tea and playing cards hadn't been invented); Roman seers 'read' the spilled guts of sacrificed animals … or sometimes sacrificed criminals. This is a practice known as 'haruspicy'. A wonderful word we should all remember in case it ever crops up in a pub quiz … which it will.†

● 'Extispicy' (not to be confused with extra-spicy) is seeing the future from anomalies in spilled guts. Another good word. The animal must be pure and sacrificed in the authorized manner. Emperor Claudius was so convinced of its value he set up a college to teach the subject.

● Emperor Augustus used 'stolisomancy' (drawing omens from the way people dress) to predict a mil-

---

* Deduct their fee? How does that work? Is it like those no-win-no-fee offers you see from ambulance-chasing lawyers these days? They beg a coin from those to whom they promise riches?
† I know because I have read it in a spilled bag of Tesco chicken giblets.

itary revolt when he saw an attendant buckling his right sandal on his left foot.

Fantastic fact ... labyrinths

Labyrinths and mazes are said to be the legacy of haruspicy. The shape of an animal's intestine could be used to predict the course of a patient's illness ... or the weather. A maze is a cobbled representation of an animal's twisting intestines. A-maze-ing.

- 'Anthropomancy' is the use of human guts – a dead virgin or child is best because they are innocent and haven't offended the gods. And (best word of all) 'splanchomancy' is what the Romans called it.

The Roman senate used haruspicy to make important decisions such as: should the Romans go to war, yes or no? It's scary to think that a small scar on a sheep's liver could mean the difference between life and death for thousands.*

We may find looking into sheep guts bizarre, but what matters is that the Romans didn't and the history of the world may have been changed forever by a kinked kidney, a crooked colon or a split spleen.

---

* The seat of the soul (the ancients believed) was the liver. Binge drinkers take note. Let's not get into 'scatomancy' (examining your own faeces) or 'uromancy' (examining someone else's pee). Not sure which is worse.

> 'Man is quite insane. He wouldn't know how to
> create a maggot yet he creates gods by the dozen.'
>
> *Anon*

Alectryomancy uses grains of corn in a circle and works like a Ouija board. Each grain is a letter and a bird (usually a cockerel) picks the grains/letters. A Roman magician used alectryomancy to discover the successor to Valens, the Roman emperor from AD 364–78. The bird pecked four grains that spelled 'T-H-E-O'. When the emperor heard of the cock's prediction, he had several persons murdered whose names began with Theo. Logical or what?

3   The quaint Christians

> 'The most heinous and cruel crimes in history have
> been committed in the name of religion.'
>
> *Anon*

The Jewish believers in the Roman Empire had a problem. Not only did they have a single god but he defined himself as a jealous god. He wouldn't let his believers worship other gods, not even a token dead sheep here or a spilt gut there.

This became a real pain when the Romans adopted emperors who in turn were worshipped as gods. Jews and Christians refused to worship the emperor-gods so were condemned as 'traitors'. The Roman punishment was to expel Jews, persecute them, destroy their places of worship and try to force the Roman gods on them. The Jews responded by rebelling (AD 66 and 115) but were generally pragmatic.

Then along came the Christian sect who felt compelled to go out and convert the world. Where Jews had kept their heads down, Christians were driven to stick their heads above the parapet. They seemed to welcome martyrdom; the Romans didn't disappoint.

There was the suspicion they'd started the Great Fire of Rome in AD 64, but there were also claims that the Christians were guilty of incest, cannibalism, eating stolen babies and sexual deviancy.* Christians went around calling one another brother or sister and kissing. How deviant is that?

Their key ceremony involved (and still does) eating the flesh of Christ and drinking his blood.

When Nero's soldiers went hunting Christian scapegoats to immolate it was often the people next door who betrayed them.†

The unfortunate victims were tied to poles, covered in tar and set alight to illuminate Nero's public gardens.‡ Other Christians were covered in animal skins and thrown to packs of wild dogs to be torn apart as the crowds cheered.

The persecution had started.

---

* Or as they say these days, 'Abstinence makes the Church grow fondlers.' Maybe they did nibble the odd neighbour in times of famine.

† Gives a whole new meaning to 'Love thy neighbour as thyself'.

‡ This is said to be the origin of the 'Roman Candle' firework. Catherine Wheels refer to Saint Catherine who converted the wife of Emperor Maxentius and was sent to be 'broken' on a wheel. The wheel itself broke (a miracle) so she was beheaded. She was never tied to a flaming wheel like her firework namesake. Having said that, she DID return a thousand years later to chat to Joan of Arc – who did go up in flames. Now you know.

4   After Nero

'Religion is the sigh of the oppressed creature, the heart of a heartless world, and the soul of soulless conditions. It is the opium of the people.'

Karl Marx (1818–83), German revolutionary socialist

When Nero died the violence against the Christians subsided. It flared intermittently over the following centuries and in different parts of the Empire. A famine here or an earthquake there? Blame the Christians. 'They upset the gods with their refusal to sacrifice,' their persecutors argued.

Emperor Trajan, who ruled from AD 98–117, received a letter from magistrate Pliny the Younger (AD 61–112) asking how to deal with a rash of complaints against Christians. A lot of reports were obviously from spiteful neighbours and Pliny thought he couldn't execute them all. He decided to compel them to sacrifice to the Roman gods, declare loyalty to Trajan and curse the name of Christ.

Trajan's decision was …

'Christianity is illegal. Members of the faith are not to be sought out; but if they are accused and convicted, they must be punished.'

Emperor Trajan (AD 53–117)

So no witch-hunt, but execute them if you can't ignore the complaints. For a hundred years after Nero there was no blanket persecution of Christians as we sometimes imagine.

The Martyrs of Lyon in AD 177 were an unfortunate exception. It was localized, not an empire-wide campaign. Emperor Marcus Aurelius was fighting for his life against the Marcomanni and Quadi tribes so was rather distracted.

The Lyon martyrs were arrested and tortured. A typical feature of any persecution was the way the victims were betrayed. Servants were arrested, feared execution, so they pointed the finger at their masters. The victims included ...

Epidosus – a clean living young man who was tortured along with his friend Alexander for his faith. They were eaten by the beasts in the local amphitheatre and 'neither uttering a groan nor a syllable, but conversing in their heart with God'. That must have been an interesting conversation.

Bishop Pothinus – a 90-year-old, so no need to execute him. The abuse in prison did that.

Ponticus was just 15 so he survived long enough to die to entertain the mob that had bayed for Christian blood.

Blandina – a frail lady (her fellow Christians said). Yet she stood up to torture so resolutely her torturers were exhausted. As a non-Roman citizen she didn't enjoy the privilege of beheading. She was tied to a stake and wild beasts were set on her. They didn't so much as nibble her. Finally she was whipped, dropped on a red-hot grate, wrapped in a net and thrown to a wild bull who tossed her into the air. The frail lady was finished off with a dagger.

Maturus – who proved impervious to torture too. When he was finally put on a heated iron seat, 'the scent of his roasted flesh filled the audience with its savour'. We all enjoy the fresh-roasted smell of a little baked buttock, but it is usually cut from a cow.

Christian corpses were thrown to the dogs and left unburied for six days. The remains were burned to ash and the ashes swept away so there would be no 'relics' for subsequent Christians to revere. That Roman mob in Lyon certainly knew how to hate.

5   Decius danger

> 'The Christian does not think God will love us because we are good, but that God will make us good because He loves us.'
>
> *C.S. Lewis (1898–1963), novelist and poet*

It was in AD 249 that the sacrifice to the gods became a legal requirement. You needed to be certified. A typical affidavit says ...

> 'I have sacrificed and tasted the sacrificial victims.'
>
> *Aurelius Digenes, resident of Alexander's Island*

In Britain today you need a driving licence to drive a car. If you find a driving test morally repugnant (or you're just plain scared) then you can get a licence without taking a test. You can send a friend to take the test or bribe the examiner.* Christians knew all the same wheezes to

---

* In 2013 it would cost you around £2,000 to bribe your way to a licence. But that particular examiner was arrested. Better resort to getting one of your slaves to do it.

dodge their test. Some sent a slave to impersonate them. If all else failed they would pay a forger, and there was a brisk trade in that business.

But martyrs like Pionius refused to dodge the Decius bullet. In Smyrna, Greece, AD 250, Pionius scolded the Roman spectators who'd come to see him die. He told them not to make fun of the weak Christians, the ones who had given in and saved themselves by making a sacrifice. He quoted Homer at them …

> 'It is not a holy thing to gloat over those who are about to die.'

He was then burned alive. We don't know if the rebuked Romans gloated over the pyrotechnic Pionius.

It's clear you didn't HAVE to die for your religion. Some Christian bishops said that eating the Roman sacrifice would bar you from the Christian Church. It was those bishops who pushed Christians through the door marked 'Martyr'.

6   Manic martyrs

> 'If Jesus came back and saw what was being done in his name, he'd never stop throwing up.'
>
> *Woody Allen (1935—), American writer, comedian*

Many Christians rushed to martyrdom as lemmings rush to throw themselves over the cliffs.* When Diocletian

---

* Which, as you know, is a lemming myth. There was a Natural Scientist Ole Worm (1588–1655) – no I didn't make that name up (or that of his father, Willum Worm) – who explained lemmings were carried on the

started to have Christians executed in AD 303 they were queuing up to die. Roman historian Eusebius said ...

> 'No sooner had the first clutch been sentenced than others, from every side, would jump onto the platform in front of the judge and declare themselves Christians. They took no account of the tortures in all their terrifying forms, but spoke boldly of their devotion to God. They received the final sentence of death with joy and laughter.'
>
> *Eusebius (AD 263–339), Roman historian*

It wasn't so much persecution as suicide. The Christians seemed determined to emulate their inspiration, Jesus.

> 'I died for you, I died for two
> I'll live for you, I'll give to you.'
> *Bee Gees lyrics 'Saved by the Bell' as not sung by Christian martyrs*

As Perpetua (the lady whom we met in the introduction) put it ...

> 'Halianus passed sentence on all of us; we were condemned to the beasts and we returned to prison in high spirits.'
>
> *Perpetua, Christian martyr*

---

wind and dropped from the sky. But it was a 1958 Disney film that showed lemmings leaping to their deaths off a Norwegian cliff that created the lemming suicide myth. They were actually Canadian lemmings, shipped in then thrown off the cliff for the cameras. Amazing what you learn from a book on the Roman Empire.

BRIEF TIMELINE

AD 64   Nero sets fire to Christians to light his public gardens.

AD 98   Emperor Trajan rules and Christianity has mushroomed through the Empire. Persecution is a bit random.

AD 177 Marcus Aurelius turns nasty. The Martyrs of Lyon suffer death for their faith.

AD 249 Emperor Dacian says sacrifice to Roman gods is a legal requirement. Christians who refuse are executed.

AD 253 Emperor Valerian singles out priests and bishops for execution.

AD 260 Gallienus proclaims tolerance for Christians throughout the Empire.

AD 303 'The Great Persecution' of Diocletian begins. The Empire is threatened on all sides and Christians become scapegoats again.

AD 305 Galerian in the Western Empire even more fierce and cruel in his persecution.*

AD 306 Emperor of the East, Constantine, has Christian leanings. By 312 he is the top man.

---

7   Holy smoke

> 'Two things are infinite: the universe and human stupidity; and I'm not sure about the universe.'
>
> *Albert Einstein*

---

* Until God sent unto him a painful disease and the emperor changed his mind.

The story of Eulalia is typical of the martyr texts that were recorded.

◆ In AD 304 Eulalia was a 13-year-old Spanish Christian. Under Diocletian's ruling she had to sacrifice to Roman gods or suffer. Her parents shut her away in their country villa to shelter her. But ...

◆ Eulalia ran off to see the Roman governor, Dacian, and bend his ear about the persecutions. He tried threats of torture to dissuade her. She spat at him and was sent to be tortured in the public forum.

◆ Soldiers used iron hooks to tear her sides and torches to burn her breasts.* Her long hair covered her modesty. As she was burned at the stake she taunted her torturers. When she died snow fell to cover her charred body.

8   Crude crucifixion

> 'When his life was ruined, his family killed, his farm destroyed, Job knelt down on the ground and yelled up to the heavens, "Why, God? Why me?" and the thundering voice of God answered, "There's just something about you that pisses me off."'
>
> *Stephen King (1947—), American novelist*

We tend to associate crucifixion with Christians but of course the Romans were using the execution method for

---

* The writers enjoyed adding spicy details of female martyrs to their accounts. They were often far more titillating than Mills and Boon. More like '50 Shades of Blood'.

hundreds of years before and after they put Jesus on a cross.

In Europe in later days they would hang people then display the body in a cage – a 'gibbet' – so they could be seen as an example.* After the Spartacus slave rebellion 6,000 survivors were crucified along the Appian Way from Rome to Capua. How many trees died to make those crosses? It would have been much less effort for the soldiers to strangle or beat or behead the victims.

But crucifixion was not just a punishment. It was, like gibbeting, a show of power *pour encourager les autres*.

Dr Peter Fox explains ...

DANGEROUS DAYS DEATH IV

CRUCIFIXION

Romans seem to have preferred nails, large iron ones. These were expensive for the time so after death they would remove them and recycle for the next crucifixion – early greens!! Insertion of nails was probably through hand/wrist into carpal tunnel or through wrist between the two main forearm bones, ulna and radius. This would give good firm fix to wood and also go through/rub against the radial nerve, thus increasing the amount of pain. At the foot end, nails would

---

* Spence Broughton was one of the last people to be gibbeted, for a highway robbery near Sheffield in 1791. His tar-preserved body stayed there for 36 years and became a popular picnic attraction. Broughton's body attracted 40,000 visitors on the first day, to the joy of the landlord of the nearest pub as it made him a fortune. Broughton's body became a local landmark, remaining in the gibbet until 1827. It was taken down when the landowner grew tired of trespassers on his land.

either go through heel bone individually into wood or the feet would be held crossed with a nail, through the ankle equivalent to wrist position of nail.

This would cause blood loss both before and after crucifixion and contribute to death from blood loss (see later).

Once you were up there on the wood, your chest would get compressed – very painful, making breathing harder.* The executioners could also add a small block of wood under the feet so you suffered longer before dying.

Death was usually from a combination of infection (wounds getting dirty from nails, flogging, etc.), hypovolaemia (blood loss, dehydration) all causing heart arrhythmias, heart failure and sometimes pulmonary emboli from clots (because you're immobile and dehydrated, clots form in vessels and break off to lungs).

Time to die would range from a few hours to days, depending on how strong you were to start with, the amount of blood loss from flogging wounds, how fast you dehydrated under the heat of the sun and whether 'friends' gave you drinks to keep you hydrated. Real friends would break your legs, to stop you supporting your upper body and help you die quicker.

Dr Peter Fox

In AD 337, Emperor Constantine I abolished crucifixion in the Roman Empire out of respect for the memory of Jesus. Up to a thousand years too late for some victims.

---

* This particularly slow and painful manner of death gave us the term 'excruciating', from the Latin meaning 'out of crucifying'.

> 'Man's inhumanity to man
> Makes countless thousands mourn.'
>
> *Robert Burns (1759–96), Scottish poet*

9   Vile vengeance

> 'God will not let any violence go unpunished, but He
> Himself will take vengeance on our enemies and will
> send home to them what they have deserved by the
> way they have treated us.'
>
> *Martin Luther (1483–1546), German monk and theologian**

In the western half of the Empire in AD 305 Emperor
Galerian enforced the worship of Roman deities and terrorized Christians.

The Christian writers positively oozed with delight at
his painful death: Emperor Galerian just oozed.

> 'Galerian was pursued by God's punishment. An
> inflammation broke out in his genitals and the disease
> ate its way incurably into his inmost bowels. From thence
> came a teeming, indescribable mass of worms and a
> sickening smell was given off. Because of his overeating
> his body was a flabby mass which decomposed and gave
> those who approached a horrifying sight.'
>
> *Eusebius*

---

* This interesting character was an expert on vengeance, of course. He
declared Jews' homes should be destroyed, their synagogues burned,
money confiscated and liberty curtailed. Luther's ideas were revived and
used in propaganda by the Nazis.

Even in the 20th century Christians were still encouraging the idea that suffering is good.

> 'I think it is very good when people suffer. To me that is like the kiss of Jesus.'*
>
> *Mother Teresa (1910–97), Albanian nun*

10   The legend of Constantine

> 'History is written by the victors.'
>
> *Winston Churchill (1874–1965), British politician and historian*

And then came Emperor Constantine who took over in AD 306. He worshipped the Unconquered Sun. That was not an official Roman god. The message it sent out was that it was fine to worship your own god or gods. Constantine was certainly tolerant of Christians.

Constantine battled against enemies of the Empire until there was only one major opponent left … usurper Maxentius. On the eve of the climactic battle Constantine had a dream. He was told that if his armies marched out under the cross of the Christians on his banner they would be victorious.

Imagine what a propaganda victory this was for the Christians. Such a triumph of faith over persecution. A miracle. God has a word in Constantine's ear and Christianity becomes his true religion.

---

* So let's get this straight, Mother Tess … when Emperor Galerian suffered a painful cancer in his genitals he was being kissed by Jesus? Interesting image.

But remember ... History is written by the victors.

And just because that story has been around 1,700 years doesn't make it any more 'true'.

> 'One of the saddest lessons of history is this: If we've been bamboozled long enough, we tend to reject any evidence of the bamboozle. We're no longer interested in finding out the truth.'
>
> *Carl Sagan (1934–96), American astronomer*

The truth? The cross is one of the symbols of the Unconquered Sun religion.

Though Constantine did not, like Saint Paul, have a vision and a sudden conversion on the road to Damascus, he *did* begin to employ Christians in his administration, and at one stage he did give his allegiance to the Christian God ... but remained vague about what it meant right up to his death.

And that's how Christian persecution ended. Not with a miracle but with a crooked cross reference.

The martyrdoms tailed away. But the victims had done the Church a great service. They were the celebs of their day, the charismatic characters we humans aspire towards. They made the Church infinitely stronger – and then the Church told them to cut out all this dying for God. 'We aren't being persecuted any longer and there are now enough saints up there to intercede for you when you get to heaven.'*

---

* In time the Church became so powerful there were few left to persecute the Christians. So they came up with a great idea to keep the faithful interested. They started persecuting one another – sect against sect, Christian killing Christian. Maybe the German philosopher Friedrich Nietzsche (1844–1900) was right when he said, 'In truth, there was only one Christian and he died on the cross.'

INSTABILITY

> The smell of a dead enemy is sweet; that of a fellow citizen even sweeter.'
>
> *Emperor Vitellius on the battlefield of his*
> *defeated predecessor Otho*

It is known as 'The Year of Four Emperors'. They were dropping like flies in a revolving door in AD 69.

So what happened to those luckless leaders Galba and Otho and Vitellius? I'm glad you asked.

— GALBA —

Emperor Galba (3 BC–AD 69)

1   Roman historian Suetonius said of Galba, 'In sexual matters he was more inclined to males, and then none but the hard bodied and those past their prime.' His cruelty was legendary – an illegal moneylender had his hands cut off and nailed to his table. A soldier who sold his rations for an inflated price was ordered to be starved to death.

2   Nero died and Galba marched on Rome. He was met by army chiefs who presented him with demands. Galba had

them killed ... not a technique recommended in many manuals on negotiating skills, but effective. When news arrived that the senate had made him emperor, Galba celebrated by having sex with the messenger.

3 Galba's supporters had promised the Praetorian Guard rich rewards if they backed the new emperor. Galba refused, saying, 'A soldier should not have to be bribed to do his job.' True, but tactless in the circumstances.

4 Galba was tight with money and determined to restore the fortunes of the Empire. More taxes. Very unpopular. Tacitus succinctly said, 'Everyone claimed he was worthy of the Empire ... until he became emperor.'

5 The German troops revolted, declared their leader Vitellius emperor and set off for Rome. The Lusitanian commander, Salvius Otho, claimed HE should be emperor and set off for Rome. Otho got there first.

6 On meeting Otho, the 71-year-old Galba bared his neck, saying, 'Strike, if it be for the good of the Romans!' They struck. The old man's head was carried to Otho. It was tossed around by his camp followers.*

Spot that emperor – Galba

Galba was 71 when he took the imperial throne. He was round-shouldered and sunken-cheeked. He had a hooked nose and limped with gout. His arthritic hands were like claws and his head as bald as a billiard ball.

---

* The honour of slicing Galba's throat was claimed by 120 soldiers. They wanted a rich reward from Otho for doing the deadly deed. New Emperor Otho had the 120 names drawn up on a list. Everyone on the list was executed. They were looking for a helping hand. But as screen actor Audrey Hepburn (1929–93) said, 'If you ever need a helping hand, it's on the end of your arm.'

– OTHO –

Galba gone, Otho on.

Emperor Otho (AD 32–69)

1   Otho was a wild young thing with a wild young wife, Pop-
    paea. Once Nero took a fancy to her Otho was divorced
    and packed off to Lusitania (Portugal). His resentment had
    ten years to fester.

2   Galba in Spain had been his neighbouring governor.
    When Galba rebelled against Nero, Otho joined him. It
    was payback time. An astrologer told Otho the omens
    said he'd come to power when Galba died. But the un-
    grateful Galba named someone else as his heir.* Galba
    had to go.

3   Wild-living Otho was short of cash and could only
    afford to bribe 23 of the Praetorian Guard to join a rebel-
    lion. The 23 persuaded their comrades to join them.
    They proclaimed Otho emperor. The omens were right in
    a way.

4   The people of Rome liked Otho because Galba had been a
    mean old man and Otho reminded them of Nero. Nero's
    statues were dug up and re-erected. Nero's lover, the
    castrated boy-bride Sporus, was reinstated as Otho's lover.
    Work on Nero's Golden Palace resumed.

5   When Otho read the state letters of the late Galba he real-
    ized how serious the Roman army rebellion in Germany
    was and set out to crush it … though the omens said he'd
    lose. The omens were right again. His army was battered

---

* Galba named a man called Piso as his heir. Otho must have been
tempted to say, 'Piso off.'

and its soldiers made friends with the German Romans.
Otho stabbed himself in the heart. His three-month reign
was over.*

Spot that emperor – Otho

There is a report that Otho was so vain he plastered his
face with bread dough, like make-up foundation, to
look good when he went into battle. It was also a depil-
atory. Suetonius described him as: 'of moderate height,
splay-footed and bandy-legged, while being almost
feminine in his care of his person. He had the hair of
his body plucked out, and because of the thinness of his
hair wore a wig carefully made and fitted to his head,
so that no one guessed he was bald. They say he used to
shave every day and smear his face with moist bread, so
as never to have a beard.'

⌐ VITELLIUS ⌐

Two gone, two to go.

Emperor Vitellius (AD 15–69)

1   Vitellius was commander of the German armies and after
    Otho attacked him (and lost) he reckoned he deserved to
    be emperor. He lasted all of eight months. He took great
    pleasure in gluttony and cruelty. Suetonius said he took

---

* It had been Roman v. Roman and Otho's sacrifice prevented a full-scale
civil war. Some of his men admired Otho's sacrifice so much that they
joined him … throwing themselves on his funeral pyre.

pleasure from inflicting death and torture on anyone for any reason. Top qualification for an emperor then.*

2   Romans were very surprised when Emperor Galba made Vitellius commander of the German legions. He was generous and matey with his officers, which made him popular, but it also proved bad for discipline. Vitellius went back a long way. He was a friend of Tiberius, who nicknamed him 'sphincter-artist'. Says it all.

3   His men proclaimed him emperor after Nero and he set off to Rome to defeat Galba. By the time he got there the throne was in the hands of Otho.† You have to go through Otho.

4   The armies of Vitellius rampaged round Rome, drinking and brawling and killing. They had extravagant arena games. The Praetorian Guard were dismissed to make way for Vitellius's own men. You can see Vitellius was not in the business of making friends. He even upset the gods ... when his priests left sacred cake for the deities, Vitellius couldn't resist pinching it for himself.

5   Vitellius heard that yet another Roman commander was on his way to take the throne. Vespasian, conqueror of Judaea, was on the march. Vitellius folded like a house of white-flag-waving cards and said, 'I abdicate!' His riotous pals deserted him. He hid in a door-keeper's dog house. He dressed in a filthy tunic to fool his executioners but his belly gave him away – it was padded with a belt full of gold coins. He was dragged out in front of the mob, who pelted him with dung. He was insulted with words like 'glutton'.

---

* A prophecy said he'd rule for a long time provided he survived his mother. No problem. He had his mother starved to death.

† When I say 'in the hands of Otho' I mean under the skinny butt of Otho. Vitellius had a much more substantial backside to fill the throne. Much more substantial.

Sticks and stones may break his bones but words could never hurt him ... the beheading probably did. The head was paraded around Rome. Now that's what you call an abdication.*

Spot that emperor – Vitellius

An obese and indolent man nicknamed 'The Glutton'. He walked with a limp as the result of a chariot accident while racing Caligula. His feasts included exotic dishes from all over the Empire: pheasant and peacock brains, pike livers and flamingo tongues. He could feast four times a day, each meal costing 400,000 sesterces.

— VESPASIAN —

The fourth and final man on the throne lasted longer.

Emperor Vespasian (AD 9–79) ...

1   This was the man sent to conquer the Jewish rebellion. He practised by battering British tribes in AD 43 then moved to Judaea. (Well it was warmer for a start.) He was popular with his troops and in the Year of Four Emperors that counted for a lot.

2   As he was beating the Jews he got news of Nero's suicide and Galba's grab for the throne. He gathered his allies and set off for Rome. It took him so long to get there he

---

* Rome had a new head. Vitellius didn't.

found there had been two emperors since Galba and was confronted by a grovelling Vitellius. Rome at last had a sensible leader to bring peace to the Empire. He saved a lot of money but spilled a lot of blood to achieve peace. Some say it cost him 50,000 lives.

3   He reformed the finances of the Empire (which sounds boring) and built the massive murder machine known as the Coliseum (which does not). His mistress Caenis was reputed to sell public offices and share the cash with Vespasian. But compared to his predecessors he was a good boy. He was lenient towards his critics. Only one, Helvidius Priscus, really riled him. At first Vespasian came up with the great put-down line, 'I will not kill a dog that barks at me.' But in the end the emperor had Priscus executed. The dog of the put-down was put down.

4   The historians were kind to Vespasian. Some said he was fated to rule ... even the statue of Julius Caesar had spun on its base to face the East where Vespasian had been campaigning. Some claimed he healed a withered hand with his spit, and cured blindness. Yet he hadn't always been so popular. In his younger days, as a commander in Rome and Tunisia, he'd failed in his duty to keep the streets clean. The locals pelted him with mud in Rome. In Tunisia he was bombarded with turnips. Swede revenge?

5   Vespasian set about expanding the Empire and making it a commonwealth in which the provinces were equal partners with Rome. The Romanization of the Empire restored the treasury. You no longer had to be a 'Man of

Rome' to be a citizen of the Empire ... and pay its taxes.*
After ten years he left the coffers full and departed with
the famous last words, 'Bear me, I appear to be turning
into a god!'†

And after the turmoil of the Year of Four Emperors there
was stability. But even then it was never boring. After all,
Vespasian had built that Coliseum and there was a lot of
danger still to be found in Rome.

---

* The cloth workers of Rome had jars outside their premises where gentlemen
could relieve themselves. The ammonia in the urine helped them to clean the
cloth. Vespasian introduced a tax on that urine. There is nothing new in the
world; to this day the tax man is still taking the piss. When Vespasian's son
Titus objected to the distasteful tax, Vespasian handed him a couple of coins
with the comment, 'Can you smell anything?'
† His end was a little more messy than that. He suffered a severe attack
of diarrhoea. A rumour said his son Titus had arranged to have his old
dad poisoned. He said, 'An emperor should die on his feet.' It is likely he
died on the toilet ... like Elvis Presley. Poisoned? Probably just 'Suspicious
Minds'. You sit there, 'Until it's time for you to go.' How appropriate, then,
that the Italian name for a urinal, *vespasiano*, was taken from Vespasian.
A reminder of his urinal tax. That's the wonder of you-rine, as Elvis didn't
sing.

INSURRECTION

— ROMAN REBELS III —
THE JEWISH REVOLT

'We know the war prepared
On every peaceful home,
We know the hells declared
For such as serve not Rome,
The terror, threats, and dread
In market, hearth and field –
We know, when all is said,
We perish if we yield.'

From 'Ulster' by Rudyard Kipling (1865–1936),
English writer and poet

Boudica and the battling Brits had been suppressed in the far north-west of the Empire. Nero the nutter was still on the throne but distracted by building a new palace and murdering anyone he took a dislike to. Still the future for the Romans looked brighter. They could see light at the end of the tunnel … of course it turned out to be an onrushing train.

The Eastern Empire (the 'Middle East to us today) was the next hot spot to erupt.

The Jewish people resented the Roman control of their lives and land. No surprise there. In AD 66, their aversion to Roman rule turned into an open revolt.

Fighting for Rome – Titus (AD 39–81) ...

> 'You cannot insult or abuse me in any way. You see, I've done nothing to deserve it. The reports must be lies, and I don't care about what is reported falsely.'
>
> *Emperor Titus*

Dad, Vespasian, had a great reputation as a fighter but it didn't run in the Flavian family. Titus's great-grandfather, Titus Flavius Petro, had been a centurion in the Roman army in 48 BC. He was best remembered for running away at the Battle of Pharsalus.* Petro proved himself a man by marrying a wealthy woman and buying his way back into Roman society. (Another lesson for us all.)

But Titus took after Vespasian and was handed the job of finishing off the campaign against the Jews.

Titus would go on to become emperor – though he only lasted 26 months. The imperial throne had gone back to keeping it in the family. By the time Titus took the throne he was generally loathed. Even Nero and Caligula had started off as popular rulers until their haloes slipped. But

---

* His commander was the great Pompey. When Julius Caesar smashed Pompey's army, Titus Flavius Petro ran away, it is true. But so did Pompey. So it's a little harsh to single out Titus's great-granddad as a coward. You fight, you lose, you run for your life. Common sense.

Titus arrived with a reputation for being cruel, greedy, ruthless and depraved.

He had a fascination for dancing boys and eunuchs but was fairly catholic in his tastes. He caused the greatest scandal in his love affair with Berenice of Judaea.

Did you know ... Berenice (born AD 28)

Berenice was a client ruler of Judaea after Titus had conquered it. She gets a bad press in the Bible. Berenice had an affair with Titus, who was 11 years her junior.* She was notorious for her love life. Her first husband died so she married her father's brother. When he died she moved to the court of her brother Herod Agrippa II and allegedly had an incestuous relationship with him. It wasn't only the Romans who liked to keep it in the family.

In AD 79 there was a plot by Alienus to depose Titus's father, Vespasian. Titus invited Alienus to dinner then ordered him to be stabbed. (You have to wonder why Alienus accepted the invite. He can't have been that hungry. Titus was already notorious for having suspected traitors executed on the spot. No, 'How do you plead?' just 'How do you bleed?')

Knowing he wasn't going to be popular as emperor he

---

* The Romans were deeply suspicious of an Eastern queen seducing one of their commanders. Cleopatra had charmed Mark Antony and that did not turn out well. Titus was persuaded to give up Berenice for the sake of the Empire. The playwrights made it out to be an heroic sacrifice. They were broken-hearted lovers, torn apart by duty. Believe that if you wish.

tried to 'buy' popularity with lavish gladiatorial games and new public baths. He also set about finishing the building of the Coliseum.

Did you know ... the Coliseum opening

The inaugural games went on for 100 days and varied from gladiatorial combat, horse and chariot races, fights between wild animals and even mock naval battles in which the theatre was flooded. Five thousand beasts died in one day. Wooden balls were thrown into the audience, in a lottery for various prizes (perhaps gold or slaves). That dreadful first day at the Coliseum was the first of many. Emperor Trajan celebrated his war wins in AD 107 with contests that featured 11,000 animals and 10,000 gladiators over 123 days. The Christian Laureolis was crucified then torn apart by a bear. How the crowds cheered.

Over the next 300 years half a million people and a million wild animals would die in the Coliseum 'games'.

Titus died in AD 81 after leaving one of his 'games'. He fell ill with a fever and died in the same house as his father. Where have you heard that story before? Yes, Emperor Augustus died in the same house as *his* father. A lesson for us all: keep away from the house where your father died and you may live forever. (Especially if you are a Roman emperor.)

There was a report that Titus fell ill with a fever. His younger brother, tired of waiting for power, suggested the best way to cure a fever was to place Titus in a box filled with snow. That chilled him then killed him.*

His last words were supposedly, 'I have made only one mistake.'† Some believe the 'mistake' was to not kill his brother Domitian.

This was the Roman who had defeated the Jews.

Fantastic fact

An old document records a disgusting legend about Titus. It says that an insect flew into the emperor's nose and ate its way into his brain for seven years. He discovered that the sound of a blacksmith hammering helped reduce the pain and arranged for blacksmiths to hammer close by. But the insect developed a resistance to the treatment and went back to gorging on the grey cells. When Titus died, his skull was opened. Inside, the insect had grown to the size of a bird. Nice.

The same pro-Jewish document has Titus making love to a prostitute, lying across some holy scrolls, as the Temple of Jerusalem burned around them.

Which rather demonstrates ...

---

* Trouble is, Domitian turned out to be a rotten emperor. The historian Suetonius wanted to show that Domitian was a wrong 'un right from the start. Suet was a retrospective character assassin. 'Emperors are a good idea,' the smarmy historian hints. 'Titus was just a bad *man*.'

† Happy the man who can die claiming that. All right, maybe not 'happy' given the circumstances. Maybe 'deluded' would be a better word. Of course Edith Piaf said she had NO regrets at all. Not even *one*, like Titus?

> 'There is no history, only fictions of varying degrees
> of plausibility.'
>
> *Voltaire (1694–1778), French philosopher*

Fighting for the rebels – Simon Bar Giora (died AD 70)

Simon led the fight against the Romans but was more a
Che Guevara guerrilla than Sir Francis Drake, repelling
the invading hordes. As the Romans marched on Jerusalem to quell the revolt against Roman rule, Simon led a
peasant army against the rear. He led the captured animals
and weapons into the city. Was he lauded as a hero? He was
not. The authorities were looking to conclude a negotiated
settlement. (Which is a bit boring.)

The Jewish establishment became Simon's target. His
fighters went around Jerusalem looting the houses of the
rich. (Well, they asked for it by licking the Roman sandals.)
Simon was accused of torturing them before murdering
them. (They didn't ask for that.)

He began to gather a large army in Judaea. The con-
servative Jews couldn't meet him in open warfare so they
captured his wife. They suggested he surrender or she
would suffer. This made him rather angry so he went to
Jerusalem, captured some citizens, cut off their hands and
sent the hands into the city with a message: Release my
wife or I'll do this to the rest of you.

They released his wife. Simon was invited into the city
to replace the despotic John of Giscala. When the Romans
arrived, Simon was captured and led off to Rome.

Fact file ... John of Giscala

'In marriage, as in war, it is permitted to take every advantage of the enemy.'
                                                    Oscar Wilde

When John of Giscala and his army were besieged he appealed to the Roman attacker Titus: 'It is the Sabbath. Can we wait till tomorrow to surrender?'

Titus agreed.

That night John of Giscala fled the city under the cover of darkness. Titus was furious. He'd been made to look a Flavian fool.*

Simon Bar Giora faced a short and messy future. So why was he risking danger and death?

The rebellion

● Gessius Florus was a greedy man. He was also the Roman governor of Judaea. He favoured the Greek residents of Jerusalem over the Jews and the Greeks began to enjoy their status as only bullies can. In AD 66 the Greeks sacrificed birds to their own gods at the entrance to the synagogue at Caesarea. This defiled the Jewish place of worship and made it ritually 'unclean'.

---

* Don't worry about Titus's bruised ego. He would get his revenge in due course. He must have been rubbing his hands in glee when John was led in chains around Rome. Maybe he said the Latin equivalent of, 'You thought you were a comedian, well you're not laughing now.'

- In a tit-for-tat gesture the temple priests stopped making sacrifices for the good of the emperor.

- The Jews asked for an audience with Gessius to lay a complaint. He charged them 8 talents to hear their plea ... then had them thrown in prison before they could say a word.

- Gessius sent in a Roman soldier to filch 17 talents from the temple in Jerusalem, for no reason other than 'the emperor needed it'. The Jewish response was unusual ... they started passing around collecting baskets to raise money for the impoverished emperor. Very funny? Gessius Florus didn't see the joke. The ringleaders were whipped then crucified.

- It was a provocation to open rebellion. The Roman garrison was overrun. The rebels captured Jerusalem and went on to control large parts of Judaea and Galilee.

- Roman troops from Syria marched towards Jerusalem. They began to attack but eventually withdrew towards the coast. Bad move. Rome's Syrian legions were massacred by Judaean nationalists. Around 6,000 died and it sent shockwaves through the Roman nation. It was even more horrific than the massacre at Teutoburg Forest almost 60 years before.

- Nero took time off from kicking wives and murdering mother to send top-gun Vespasian to sort out the rebels. Vespasian was joined by his son Titus. Vespasian was patient. He rolled up the Jewish strongholds one at a time, starting in Galilee and heading for Jerusalem.

- By AD 67 he had restored Roman control to Galilee and the Mediterranean coastal cities. In AD 68 he marched on to Jericho and that just left Jerusalem. Then he stopped. He had a slightly bigger fish to fry. Nero was dead (loud cheers) and Galba became the new emperor.

- But the Empire was in turmoil and was about to enter a year of civil war known as the Year of the Four Emperors. Emperors Galba and Otho hopped the twig in quick succession and Vitellius became emperor in April AD 69.

- Vitellius was not the choice of the armies in Egypt and Judaea, who declared Vespasian emperor. Vespasian returned to Rome to claim the emperor's crown that was foretold in the stars. Was Judaea saved? No. When Vespasian became the new emperor he ordered his son Titus to finish the job in Judaea. Which he did. 'Go for it, son.'

The end

'To the victor belong the spoils. In a war or other contest, the winner gets the booty.'
Senator William Learned Marcy of New York (1786–1857) *

Titus decided to besiege Jerusalem. (Vespasian had been against that.) A new broom proved effective. The brutality

---

* Marcy was using a metaphor. He was saying that when administration won a US election, thousands of public servants were sacked and members of the winning party took over their jobs. But of course to the Romans it was literal. You lose the battle? You lose your treasures.

of Titus against the conquered Judaean towns drove refugees into Jerusalem. Up to a million crowded inside its walls. More mouths to feed, less strength to withstand a blockade.

Titus came up with a smart plan. He dug a trench around the city and built his own wall as high as the city walls. Anyone trying to escape Jerusalem was trapped in the trench and crucified. There were as many as 500 crucifixions a day. The victims could be seen from the city walls and the effect on Jewish morale must have been devastating.*

The tactics of the defending commanders were curious. They burned supplies of dried food to encourage the hungry population to fight. Risk dying in a fight, or risk dying of starvation? Many starved.

On 10 August AD 70 the Romans set fire to the temple. The temple was destroyed and the treasures stolen. A Jewish historian, Josephus (AD 37–100), excused Titus.† He said the soldier that started it had acted against the emperor's express orders.

> 'The search for a scapegoat is the easiest of all hunting
> expeditions.'
>
> *Dwight D. Eisenhower (1890–1969), US President*

---

* At the same time you have to wonder what the crucified were thinking of. Surely after the first 100 were displayed the remaining 400 would get the message? Samuel Johnson described a second marriage as 'the triumph of hope over experience'. I wonder what he made of the 102nd crucifixion.

† No, that is not a misprint. Josephus was a Jewish fighter, defeated in the war. He defected to the Romans, said the Jewish Messianic prophecies predicted Vespasian would become emperor, and then became a best buddy of Vespasian's son Titus. Turn-coat or turn-toga?

The temple would never be rebuilt. Rubbing in the insult to Jewish sensitivities, the Romans conducted sacrifices to the Roman eagle standards in the temple precincts.

In September AD 70, Titus finally completed the capture of Jerusalem. The siege had lasted a cruel 140 days but Titus wasn't planning on going anywhere else.

The table of the showbread and the temple's golden furniture was packed off to Rome. Titus celebrated the birthday of his father in Caesarea Maritima. He then celebrated the birthday of little brother Domitian in Berytus. Now *you* may celebrate a birthday with cake and candles or even a drop of champagne. Titus celebrated in blood. He had thousands of Jewish rebel prisoners slaughtered.

> 'They perished in combats with wild beasts or in fighting one another or in being burned alive.'
>
> *Josephus*

Most rebels abandoned the cause, realizing it was hopeless, while still others fought in fortresses that were later taken by the Romans.

Simon Bar Giora was dragged to the forum with a halter round his neck – a sign of his humiliation. He was scourged with whips, to prolong the agony. Finally he was executed by being thrown off the Tarpeian Rock. A wonderful spectacle for all concerned, public executions always being a favourite blood sport of the Roman people. What does Dr Fox have to say about death at the Tarpeian Rock?

DANGEROUS DAYS DEATH V

TARPEIAN ROCK

I would imagine before being flung off you would feel quite anxious – heart racing, sweaty, breathing fast – knowing what was to come.

You can die from even minor falls but accepted wisdom is that over 10 metres (30 feet) is a good discriminator for serious injury and probable death, so a fall from the 24-metre (80-foot) Tarpeian Rock spells almost certain death.

As you start to fall you accelerate under the force of gravity, wind rushing through your hair, clothes flapping. A 10-metre fall means you hit the ground at around 22 mph; 24 metres means speed at ground arrival is around 60 mph. So once above 10 metres you don't get much added death from higher falls. In fact, once above around 160 metres you don't fall any faster if you do go higher.

As to what happens as you hit ground … the body decelerates practically instantaneously. Instant loss of consciousness, bones fracture – especially the spine in thoracic/cervical region, pelvis and legs. Internal organs tear and bleed. The aorta commonly tears under the deceleration and you bleed internally very quickly, blood pressure drops, heart stops, resulting in death.

So not a bad way to go, nice flight (albeit one-way), good views and a very quick, one would say painless, end.

Dr Peter Fox

The revolt wasn't quite over. The near impregnable fortress at Màsada held out until AD 73. When a relative of Titus, Flavius Silva, stormed the citadel, the defenders killed themselves rather than be captured. If the alternative was to be burned alive, eaten alive or thrown off a rock alive, it's hard to blame them.

Did you know ... Masada

There were just seven survivors of the siege of Masada in south-east Israel – five children and two women. The other 96 men, women and children cried, 'Death before slavery' ... and then died to prove they believed it.

King Herod had built the place 40 years before and it was probably the greatest fortress in the world.

Titus started to wall in Masada as he had Jerusalem. The Romans used Jewish prisoners to build a great ramp out of earth and stones. After a year it was right up to the walls.*

The Romans charged up the ramp and smashed down the walls. The defenders tried to barricade the gap with wood but the legionaries burned it away.

Josephus talked to the survivors and described what happened. Jewish leader Eleazar ben Yair told the men to draw lots and Eleazar chose the ten who would kill the other 957.

---

* It appears cruel that the Romans used Jewish prisoners as slave labour to build the ramps that would defeat their compatriots. But *were* they compatriots? The Masada fortress was garrisoned by a group known as Zealots who had wandered around Jerusalem in the earlier days of the war, assassinating anyone considered to be a collaborator. It was a reign of terror. They were the ones who burned the food to encourage the rest of the besieged to fight. Were the Jewish ramp labourers enthusiastic? Zealous against the Zealots?

The ten who were left would be killed one by one and then the last man would kill himself. A caring mother took her children and hid in a drain.

We don't know what happened to the seven survivors of the Masada suicide pact.

Don't feel too sorry for the men who died at Masada. They were members of a fanatical group known as the 'Zealots'. When the revolt against the Romans started in AD 54 the Zealots turned to terrorism and assassination and became known as 'Sicarii' (from the Greek word meaning 'dagger men'). They roamed through public places with hidden daggers to strike down people who were friendly to Rome.

In 1965 the fortress at Masada was excavated by archaeologists and they found pieces of pottery with Jewish names scratched on them. These could have been the names drawn out of the hat to decide who would do the killing. Creepy.

Did you know ... the Tarpeian Rock

Traitors and deserters from the Roman army were often punished by being thrown from the Tarpeian Rock in Rome. In AD 214 alone 370 deserters were thrown from the place. Tiberius had a poet, Aelius Saturninus, thrown off the Tarpeian Rock for penning an insulting verse.

What did Tiberius chant as the poet took the dive?

'Roses are red, violets are blue, Aelius naughty, so Aelius flew'?

CALM

'If a man were called to fix a period in the history of the world, during which the condition of the human race was most happy and prosperous, he would without hesitation name that which elapsed from the death of Domitian to the accession of Commodus.'

Edward Gibbon (1737–94), English historian and MP,
author of The History of the Decline and Fall of the
Roman Empire

Mr Gibbon ended his book by concluding the Romans became effeminate and succumbed to the big butch barbarians. Not everyone agrees, but it was a theory that was adopted by school books for 250 years.

Did you know – Edward Gibbon

Gibbon once compared his finishing a book to giving birth to a baby. They are both the result of labour, I suppose.

Eddie said that the Church's histories of the Roman Empire exaggerated the number of martyrs who died for the religion. This did not go down well with the Church, who called him a 'paganist'.

Now Mr Gibbon may be a great historian. But that sort of 'happy and prosperous' statement has to be challenged. Prosperous? Preposterous. It was only 'happy and prosperous' for a select group. Don't worry, for those of us interested in the 'miserable and poor' there was still an enormous amount of death and destruction, melancholy and wretchedness. As with any 'golden age' in history, it all depends upon who you were.

From the end of the Jewish Revolt till the reign of Marcus Aurelius in AD 180 there was relative peace. The *pax Romana*. Yes, there was another revolt in Judaea from AD 132 to 135 with massive destruction and loss of life. But apart from *that* there was relative peace. Then there was the awful Emperor Domitian who followed Titus. But apart from *that* there was relative peace.

BRIEF TIMELINE

AD 69 The Year of Four Emperors. Says it all really. Galba, Otho and Vitellius live by the sword and die by the sword ... literally. Vespasian comes to stay for ten years.

AD 74 The Jewish revolt finally ends with the bloody destruction of the last stronghold at Masada.

AD 79 Vespasian dies. Son Titus takes over. Vesuvius erupts and buries Pompeii. Archaeologists celebrate the petrified evidence. Petrified Pompeian people don't.

AD 80 Titus opens the Coliseum. Formal dress (togas) required. Gladiators are the stars, animals the exotica, Christians the pet food.

AD 81 Titus dies, possibly of plague. Deadly Domitian

(Vespasian's second son) takes over.

AD 83 Brit governor Agricola (AD 40–93) marches into Scotland to crush the Caledonians. Agricola's son-in-law, Tacitus, reports that 10,000 Scots die to 360 legionaries. Believe that if you wish.* Agricola's reward is to be recalled to Rome by the jealous Emperor Domitian.

AD 85 Those Dacians in the Balkans are revolting again. Governor Sabinus is murdered and his legion massacred. Domitius himself leads the rescue-revenge.

AD 89 Plot against Emperor Domitian by Saturninus. It fails but the fallout is nasty as Domitian's tolerant rule turns cruel.

AD 90 Domitian has expelled the philosophers from Rome. Now he begins a purge of anyone who opposes him.† The tribes of northern Germany are finally pacified.

AD 92 Yet again the Dacians are revolting.

AD 96 Domitian is assassinated, thank goodness. Nerva takes his place for a couple of years, then …

AD 98 … Trajan takes the imperial throne. A career soldier at the helm … again. The new emperor is fond of wine and young boys … again.

AD 106 Those Dacians are finally crushed and their king, Decebalus, cuts his own throat. The Romans finish the job the king started and remove the whole head.

---

* No one is sure where the battle took place. Some even argue it NEVER took place. But Tacitus would not invent a battle – not even for his father-in-law – because it would risk his reputation if it was proved false. He would lose his street cred … not to mention his Watling Street cred.

† Torture by applying flames to the genitals is a favourite of Domitian, who did NOT write the song 'Great Balls of Fire'. But maybe he should have.

It is thrown down the Gemonian stairs.*
AD 117 Hadrian becomes emperor and the Brits finally get
    a wall to keep out some tartan terrors to the north.
    Especially the Attacotti.

Fact file ... the Attacotti

The Attacotti lived near Glasgow. St Jerome wrote
(around AD 410) ...
'A fearless tribe of Scotland, the Attacotti, are accused of
enjoying the taste of human flesh. When they hunted
the woods for prey, it is said that they attacked the
shepherd rather than his flock. They curiously selected
the brain, both of males and females, which they cooked
for their horrid meals.'†

So who was this Deadly Domitian?

— DOMITIAN (AD 51–96) —

'History: An account, mostly false, of events
unimportant, which are brought about by rulers
mostly knaves, and soldiers mostly fools.'

Ambrose Bierce

---

* Decebalus was a nickname meaning 'Man with the strength of ten
wild animals'. That must have made it ten times harder to cut his own
throat.
† The story could be apocryphal. The legend that the Attacotti caught
and fried Mars Bars alive (in batter) is certainly untrue.

Titus had named his brother Domitian as his heir. In Imperial Rome this is usually an invitation for your heir to bump you off. Titus died of a fever and the gossips said it was poison. But the gossips always said that. The only thing to support it is that the new emperor, Domitian, turned out to be every bit as vicious as Nero or Caligula. So he was *capable* of murdering big bruv.

He started as he meant to go on by insisting everyone address him as 'master and god'. (We've all had a teacher like that at some time.)

Domitian took on the role of 'Censor' in AD 84 which meant having an overview of Roman morals … especially the investigation of sex scandals. This is like a fox appointing himself head of the chicken coop. He could enjoy the veniality of his fellow Romans while having no one to watch over his own debauchery. He was attracted to eunuchs and as a young man had been the lover of a couple of senators. He lived in an illicit relationship with his niece, Julia, and forced her to abort their baby. That killed her, but he had coins portraying her ascending to heaven on the back of a peacock … so that was all right then. Maybe not everyone's ideal choice to sit in judgement on Roman morals. But he was Domitian's choice and that was all that mattered.

> 'Nearly all men can stand adversity, but if you want to test a man's character, give him power.'
>
> *Abraham Lincoln (1809–65), US President*

As he set out to expand the Empire, the army and the people loved him. The upper classes, the targets of his voyeurism, were not so loving.

One of his 'investigations' led to a couple of Vestal Virgins being found guilty of impropriety ... basically they would have contravened a Roman Trades Descriptions act by calling themselves 'Virgins'. They were buried alive. Their lovers were beaten to death with rods.* The Romans found it distasteful. Not a display of propriety, more a needless display of callousness.

That callousness showed itself in his black humour. On one occasion he had a room in his palace painted black and blackened boys served black food to the invited senators. He presented each guest with a stone carved with his name and shaped like a gravestone. The senators went home, expecting imminent execution. When the dreaded knock came on the door they found they were presented with the jokey but expensive grave gifts from the banquet. The boys, nicely scrubbed, delivered them and were available for the senators' use ... or abuse.

How hilarious was that? Oh how the senators must have laughed.

Did you know ... Domitian's palace

It was said that Domitian's palace was built of marble so shiny it was like a mirror. This would enable the emperor to have 360-degree vision and ensure no one could sneak up behind to stab him in the back. Ironic then that he died in the palace – stabbed from the front.

---

* As a guardian of the nation's morals he made Mary Whitehouse look like a pussy cat.

The good ...

> 'Domitian never took the trouble to study history.'
>
> *Suetonius*

It's the familiar Roman story of the people becoming dis-illusioned with their emperor after his promising start, plotting to kill him and eventually succeeding. Déjà-vu all over again, as they say, because he learned nothing from the lives of the previous emperors.

■ He was a touch obsessive about attending to the details of government. He wanted it done 'right'. The Romans loved his magnificent building schemes, his pure silver coins and, of course, his desire to rule the whole of the known world. What's good for the emperor's good for the Romans.

■ The Chatti tribe lived across the Rhine from Rome's border in Gaul. They'd been involved in the massacre of Augustus's legions in AD 9 and were a tough nut to crack. They were organized and planned campaigns rather than raids. Domitian's legions subdued them but it wasn't a comprehensive defeat. He celebrated it as a victory. No one was impressed, least of all the historians, like Dio, who sneered that Domitian went to war yet never saw a blow struck in anger. The enemy were certainly not cowed.

> 'Other Germans go into battle. The Chatti make war.'
>
> *Tacitus*

■ Domitian kept the plebs happy with his spectacular games in the Coliseum and other arenas. A naval battle was fought in a flooded arena. That was nothing new. Claudius had held a sea battle on Lake Fucinus with two dozen trireme ships. That was the famous occasion when the criminals turned to him and cried, 'We who are about to die salute you.' Because they WERE going to fight to the death ... their deaths ... and were trying to suck up to the emperor. Claudius replied, 'Or not.' The criminals interpreted that as a pardon and refused to fight. Claudius had to hobble along the shore shouting and threatening and making promises before eventually having the rebels chopped and burned. The 'We who are about to die salute you' cry isn't recorded anywhere else, yet we tend to think of it as something gladiators said every time they entered the arena. Another myth. Domitian's naval battle had no such problem with rebels but he did manage to upset the crowds – he started reading his official papers rather than watch the action. Unforgivable.

■ He was also said to have staged fights between female gladiators and midgets – but he always 'arranged' for the dwarf to win the fight. Domitian had a fascination with the idea of fighting women. As historian Cassius Dio (AD 150–235) said, 'the women drove horses, killed wild beasts and fought as gladiators, some willingly and some sore against their will.'

One of the freak-shows the Romans enjoyed was watching women fight in the arenas as gladiators. But the Roman poets scorned it. Everyone a critic …

'See how she slashes at dummies of wood,
As she trains for the fighting, she is simply no good.

See how the helmet just weighs down her head,
Though there's really no chance that she'll end up real dead.

Why does she fight? Does she think she's a bloke?
Her husband should tell her she looks like a joke.

The bandages thick make her legs look like trees,
We laugh when she trips and falls down on her knees

Panting and groaning with sweat on her face,
She only brings women pure shame and disgrace.'*

Juvenal (c. AD 60–140), Roman poet

The bad …

■ Domitian strove for novelty in his 'games'. In addition to gladiatorial contests between women and dwarfs, his innovations included a category of glad-

---

* A clear message to all women readers. It is acceptable to enter the arena and be torn apart by a bear or a bore. But to mimic a manly pursuit like gladiatorial combat is demeaning and vulgar. Don't do it. Curiously, women boxers are viewed with distaste today. Ages change, some people don't.

iator known as Anadabatae, who fought blindfolded. A 'games master' whipped reluctant warriors to fight harder. His helpers came into the arena after a fight to stop any cheating. One was dressed in a tight tunic, wore soft leather boots and a mask that gave him the nose of a hawk. He carried a big hammer and represented Dis, ruler of the underworld. His job was to smash the loser's head in to make sure he was dead. In front of Dis is another man with wings on his helmet and carrying a red-hot poker. He represented Mercury, messenger of the gods, there to jab the victim with the poker to see if he moved.

■　Some victims were dressed in golden clothes and had to dance happily for the crowd. Then their clothes would be set on fire and it became a grim dance of death. Artists built forests in the arena to make wild animals look at home. Men with spears, flaming torches, daggers, bows and arrows hunted and slaughtered bears, lions, bulls, panthers, leopards and tigers. Sometimes animals were set to fight other animals – bear against buffalo, buffalo against elephant, and elephant against rhino.

> 'The Coliseum is steeped in the blood of the early Christians who had died for their religion.'*
>
> *Lord Byron*

■　The Roman general Saturninus was dissatisfied enough to lead a rebellion. He'd seen how Vitellius

---

* Mind you, Byron drank wine from a human skull so he's a right one to talk.

had marched the German legions to Rome 20 years before and decided he could do the same.* Saturninus held the savings of his armies and robbed the pot of money to pay for his rebellion. Domitian's forces defeated him, then the retribution started. Rebels were hunted down and executed. Domitian had no proof that any senators were involved so there was no purge of the upper classes. Maybe he should have learned from history and looked a little closer to home?

And the mad ...

■ Domitian was weird. Yes, *most* Roman emperors were weird but Domitian was seriously twisted. He liked catching flies, stabbing them with the point of a pen and tearing their wings off. And a top tip for sycophants ... don't mention his bald head. Even when he had portraits painted the artists showed him with flowing locks. That's what is called artistic licence.†

■ It seems Domitian had an aversion to artists of the theatrical kind. When a pantomime actor called Paris seduced the empress, Domitian killed him in the street. Just for good measure he killed Paris's apprentice actor. The boy's crime was to look and act like Paris. Oh yes he did.

---

* If Saturninus had had a better history teacher he'd have been told Vitellius's stay on the emperor's throne was very short and ended messily for the usurper. Maybe Saturninus DID know that. But some people (we've all met them) think they know better. Saturninus ended bloodily without even the pleasure of parking his butt on the throne.
† It is also called 'knowing on which side your bread is buttered' or 'knowing the best way to avoid painful execution'.

■ As Domitian became increasingly paranoid he began executing people for intellectual reasons rather than for treason. And he definitely lost his sense of humour. Writers who criticized him were executed. One senator was executed for 'impiety' and another for 'atheism'. A relation of the toppled emperor, Otho, dared to have a posthumous birthday party for his kinsman and was executed.

The end

Domitian said that no one would believe the plots against him until one of them succeeded. Which puts us in mind of Spike Milligan …

> *'Duirt mé leat go raibh mé breoite'* (Irish for 'I told you I was ill')*
>
> *Spike Milligan*

Domitian would be able to say 'I told you they were out to get me' in the few minutes of his struggle with his assassins.

It was a carefully devised plan, possibly initiated by Domitian's wife. His trusted chamberlain Parthenius, obviously worried that his days were numbered after the emperor executed his secretary, Epaphroditus, in a fit of paranoia, organized the plot. It was to be carried out by

---

* The local church authorities refused to allow 'I told you I was ill' on the headstone. Milligan had it written in Irish and it was allowed. The headstone was removed to allow the interment of his wife and sadly never replaced. If we can't laugh at death then what can we laugh at?

Parthenius's freedman, Maximus, and a steward called Stephanus, who pretended to be injured so he could smuggle in a dagger beneath his bandages.

The doors had been locked so they wouldn't be interrupted and Domitian's sword had been removed from its usual position beneath his pillow. It was High Noon. Domitian was always twitchy at midday because an astrologer had said he would die at noon.

'What time is it?' Domitian asked a serving boy.

The boy, who was part of the plot, replied, 'More than an hour afternoon, Master and God.'

Domitian relaxed and settled down with his official papers. Stephanus was hurried into the emperor's presence with urgent news of a conspiracy. Paranoid Domitian let Stephanus in, little suspecting the conspiracy was in his own back yard.

Stephanus stabbed Domitian in the groin.* The emperor and his attacker wrestled on the ground for a while before the other servants, including a gladiator, finished the emperor off. It was noon.

His body was carted off on a bier like a commoner and quickly burned, emperor or no emperor. As the US Declaration of Independence didn't say: 'All men are cremated equal.'

Senators celebrated and gleefully expunged his name from the public monuments he'd built. That was an ignominy shared only by Nero.

The next emperor was shuffled onto the throne. Quickly. Suspiciously quickly, as if the senate had an inkling that Domitian's noons were numbered.

---

* Male readers may at this point wish to pause and take a handkerchief as their eyes are surely watering. It was reported by historian Suetonius that Domitian 'stood in a state of amazement'. Well, with a sword stuck in your groin you do tend to, don't you?

CATACLYSM

— ROMAN DISASTER II —
VESUVIUS

> 'Tragedy. Here I lie in a lost and lonely part of town.'
>> *'Tragedy' sung by the Bee Gees (1979)*

> 'I plead for my life! I plead for justice! ... Oooh I'm a miserable pleader!'
>> *Frankie Howerd (1917–92), British comedian*
>> *in TV series* Up Pompeii

Titus may have ruled for just 26 months but the gods were not smiling on him. They visited plague and fire and disaster like some Biblical curse.

The plague hit Rome and then another devastating fire swept through the city. Nero wasn't even around to play the lyre this time.

Titus saw it as a bad omen and sure enough he didn't last long.

But the most spectacular and defining moment of his reign was the destruction of Pompeii (and Herculaneum) when Vesuvius erupted on 24 August 79. Titus had been on the throne just two months when the volcano popped its cork.

Thousands died horrible deaths at Pompeii and Herculaneum. Yet visitors find it attractive.

> 'Many disasters have befallen the world, but few have brought posterity so much joy.'
>   *Johann Wolfgang von Goethe (1749–1832), German poet*

Joy? The graveyard of 60,000 people? Archaeologists rejoiced 1,700 years after Vesuvius erupted and they are still rejoicing.* A slice of Roman life had been preserved in ash so that 2.5 million ghoulish tourists can visit every year to gloat over the mass graves that are Pompeii and Herculaneum.†

What happened?

● The first hint was an earthquake that rattled the town. But the Romans had no seismologists to tell them this could stir Mount Vesuvius into life. The

---

* A 2013 BBC documentary presenter described Pompeii as an 'exciting' and a 'magical' place. Of course making tens of thousands of people vanish in minutes is indeed a good 'magical' trick. Making them rise again from the ashes at the end of the act would be a truly astonishing act.

† Which is not as grim as the Pompeians themselves who went to WATCH people in the act of dying in their execution arenas. But it is still a curious way to spend an Italian holiday. Sun, sea, sand and skeletons.

place does seem to have suffered from ash falls and mudslides in the preceding centuries. Just 17 years before the big bang of AD 79 there had been earth tremors and 600 sheep died in noxious air, probably volcanic carbon dioxide. The folk of Pompeii did not flock away. Many stayed to rebuild, some moved to safer cities.

But in the AD 62 quake the shattered oil lamps started fires. People starved, anarchy ruled.

Any respectable insurance company would slap a hefty premium on your pad in Pompeii.

● On 20 August 79 small earthquakes shook the towns and grew stronger each day. Still there was no Pompeii panic or Herculaneum horror.

> 'Earth tremors were not particularly alarming because they are frequent in Campania.'
>
> *Pliny the Younger (AD 61–112), Roman lawyer and writer*

● The festival of Vulcanalia, the god of fires AND volcanoes, fell on 23 August. Maybe someone upset Vulcan. The priests certainly didn't read the sacrificial entrails very well or they'd have been packing their bags. The next day Vesuvius erupted. A 20-mile plume rose into the air and for 12 hours the locals watched it and suffered the ash-fall. It was uncomfortable but they didn't see it as dangerous.

They were wrong. The rising gases and plasma collapsed and created a pyroclastic wave of enormous heat and speed that raced towards them. It hit Herculaneum with a blast of heat that stripped the flesh from the citizens in moments. The brains boiled and blew the skulls open. It was mercifully quick.

Pompeii, ten miles away survived that first blast of heat and people failed to take the window of opportunity and make a run for it.

> 'Learn this: while I am alive, you, hateful death, are coming.'
>
> *Pompeii graffiti*

Pliny the Younger's uncle was Pliny the Elder (AD 23–79), a prefect of the Roman navy. The Elder was based across the bay from Pompeii at Misenum. He was to die in a heroic but futile rescue attempt – maybe.

On 24 August 79, he was getting ready to cross the Bay of Naples. When he wasn't running the navy he was a naturalist. To witness a volcanic eruption at close quarters was something to die for … except he didn't imagine that would be quite so literal.

As he set sail he received a message from his friend Rectina pleading for rescue. He sent the great oared galleys to help with the evacuation. But he himself set off on a small sailing 'cutter' to reach Rectina. Big mistake. Pliny the Younger (who wrote about Uncle Pliny's death using accounts from the survivors) decided not to join the trip across the bay. Pliny-the-one-with-his-head-screwed-on.

As Uncle Pliny's little boat neared Pompeii, hot ash began to fall on it. Pliny's helmsman advised turning back, to which Pliny replied: 'Fortune favours the brave, steer to Pompeii!'

Death, as well as fortune, is rather fond of the brave.

The rescuers landed and found the town 'in the greatest confusion'. Pliny hugged and comforted his old mate. They loaded the little cutter but the same winds that blew the boat to Pompeii stopped it from leaving.

In the words of Pliny the Younger ...

> 'Ash was now falling on the ships, darker and denser the closer they went. It fell along with rock that was blackened and burned and broken by fire. The sea was becoming clogged and debris from the volcano was blocking the shore. He paused for a moment wondering whether to turn back ...'

In the (likely) words of Pliny the Elder, 'Oooops!'

He was trapped. Uncle Pliny waited for the wind to change but in the end feared the never-ending ash would force the houses to collapse. They set off on foot.

Pliny's friends later reported that he sat down and could not get up. He was left behind. Those dear friends – the ones he'd come to rescue – reported that he'd been overcome by the same volcanic gases that had killed the sheep 17 years before. Humbug ... baa humbug you might say. If the gases killed Uncle Pliny then why didn't it kill the friends? When they went back three days later (26 August) they found he was fossilized under hardened ash.*

---

* An alternative version from Suetonius says Uncle Pliny was not a fallen hero. He says that the chubby chap approached the shore as a natural history observer. When the heat from the volcano struck, he begged a slave to kill him to make a quick end. The story of Uncle Pliny as a hero came from nephew Pliny in a letter written more than 20 years after the eruption. Was the nephew trying to gild the memory of his uncle? Would you?

The truth is Uncle Pliny was corpulent and asthmatic. Who ate all the pies?*

Pliny the Elder's death is explained by Dr Fox as follows ...

DANGEROUS DAYS DEATH VI

VOLCANIC GASES

Poisonous gases given off by volcanic eruptions include sulphur dioxide, carbon dioxide and hydrogen sulphide. Sulphur dioxide smells of sulphur, carbon dioxide is odourless and hydrogen sulphide smells of bad eggs, so I would assume that sulphur dioxide killed him as witnesses reported smelling sulphur.

When breathed in, sulphur dioxide dissolves very readily in your lungs to form sulphurous acid, which is a severe irritant. The tubes in the lungs constrict, making it harder to breathe and the epiglottis (at the back of your throat) closes, blocking your airway. Unable to breathe, you suffocate, fighting for breath as every part of your body cries out for oxygen. Your heart runs out of oxygen first. Once it stops, no blood is pumped round your body. Starved of blood and oxygen, your brain cells start to die. Fortunately this means you lose consciousness, so you miss the final few minutes when your brain (and you) finally die.

Dr Peter Fox

---

* Excavations in Herculaneum unearthed coprolites – fossilized faeces. On examining them, scientists learned about the diet of the locals and found they ate a lot of fish – heads and all. Who ate all the eyes?

Pliny the Younger, in the comparative safety across the bay, ran off as the dark cloud blotted out the sun. He later said …

> 'I said we should leave the road while we could still see, or be knocked down and trampled underfoot in the dark by the crowd behind.
>
> We had scarcely sat down to rest when darkness fell, not the dark of a moonless or cloudy night, but as if the lamp had been put out in a closed room.
>
> You could hear the shrieks of women, the wailing of infants, and the shouting of men; some were calling their parents, others their children or their wives, trying to find them by their voices.
>
> Many cried for the gods to help, but others said there were no gods left, and that the world had been plunged into darkness for evermore.'

The whole town disappeared under the ash and was forgotten. Then, in the 1700s, it was discovered by archaeologists. The diggers found old Roman graffiti on the walls that said …

> 'Gaius Pumidius Dipilus was here, 3 October 78 BC.'✱
>
> 'To the one defecating here. Beware of the curse. If you look down on this curse, may you have an angry Jupiter for an enemy.'

✱ Obviously they didn't use the abbreviation 'BC' because the way of measuring years from the birth of Christ hadn't been devised. They measured from the supposed foundation of Rome – 79 BC is the modern equivalent.

'Auge loves Allotenus.'

'I screwed the barmaid.'

'Virgula to her boyfriend Tertius: You're disgusting!'

'Weep, you girls. My penis has given you up. Now it penetrates men's behinds. Goodbye, wondrous femininity!'

'Chie, I hope your haemorrhoids rub together so much that they hurt worse than when they ever have before!'

'Samius to Cornelius: go hang yourself.'

'Theophilus, don't perform oral sex on girls against the city wall like a dog.'

'We have pissed in our beds. Host, I admit that we shouldn't have done this. If you ask: Why? There was no potty.'

'Celadus the Thracian gladiator makes the girls moan.'

'On April 19th, I made bread.'

Echoes of Facebook these days? As a poetic piece of graffiti says:

'I wonder, Wall, why you don't crash,
You bear the weight of all this trash.'
Pompeii graffiti – wall of the Basilica

Yes, the writer definitely had Facebook in mind.

> In Herculaneum, ten miles nearer to Vesuvius, there have been 340 skeletons unearthed so far. Huddled in the boatsheds on the beach are mainly women and children. On the shoreline the skeletons are mostly male.

A volcano throws out rock so hot it is liquid, steam so hot it is above the usual 100 degree Centigrade boiling point and gases that can reach 800 degrees F.

Lava flows downhill from a volcano. But it was the superheated gas and ash that did the damage. As many as 12 pyroclastic surges hit Herculaneum. Not that there was anyone left to count surges 2 to 12.

These pyroclastic surges are gaseous enough to ride over ridges and travel far further, far hotter, far faster. An Italian sports car like a Ferrari could not have outrun the 200 to 290 mph surge. The prancing horse would be a prancing skeleton in an instant. And Ferraris weren't available to even the richest Herculaneans.

If lava had started running towards Pompeii they'd have escaped much sooner. The cloud of smoke that turned night into day was ten miles over their heads and seemed to pose no danger. They couldn't see the hot gases because they came from the *base* of the eruption.

For those of an anorak persuasion the statistics are awesome.*

---

* And for those who are NOT of an anorak persuasion they are still awesome. You may never have spotted a train in your life, but you'd be astonished at the force of nature.

- ✦　1.5 million tons of volcanic material was thrown up every second.

- ✦　Vesuvius generated 100,000 times the thermal energy of the Hiroshima bombing.

- ✦　The column rose to over 20 miles. And what goes up must come down.

- ✦　The shoreline was extended 400 metres into the bay with the new material falling. It remains there today.

- ✦　Twelve layers of ash measuring 25 metres in depth swallowed Pompeii.

As the heavier cinders and ash fell, most of the people of Pompeii tried to escape. But worse was to come. A secondary pyroclastic surge hit them, cooler than at Herculaneum but carrying enough rock and debris to crush and bury the Pompeians. Even a 'cold' surge (where the lava comes in contact with a lake or bay) has poisonous gases like hydrogen sulphide (the 'rotten egg' gas). Who wants to die smelling like a sewer?

It used to be thought that the Pompeians suffocated under the ash cloud. Research from 2010 now says it was heat from the pyroclastic surge that caused them to hop the twig.

> 'Once you are dead, you are nothing.'
>
> *Pompeii graffiti*

Weirdest of all, it is not just the suffocation story that is under fire ... no pun intended, but laugh if you wish.

Reports that the eruption occurred on 24 August 79 have recently been challenged. It's only Pliny's letter that gives that date. Historians argue that archaeological evidence points to a November eruption:

1   The victims appear to be wearing heavier, winter clothing than they would in August.
2   The summer fruits in the shops were being sold as dried fruit ... as it would when summer is a distant memory.
3   The vegetables are of the type you'd expect to find in the shops from October onwards.
4   Wine-fermenting jars were sealed, as they would be in October.
5   Coins feature Titus with a title that was only given to him in September 79.

So 24 August or 23 November? One of those was a dangerous day in imperial Pompeii.

Hot air

While the pyroclastic surge may have killed a majority in Pompeii and Herculaneum there were some who suffered suffocation.

For 250 years the terrible tourists have come to delight in death. But it hasn't always been easy for them to see the whole truth. Many of the frescoes and artefacts were fertility symbols – large phallic representations to encourage the gods to bring burgeoning life to the fields and gardens (and bedrooms).

They were seen as embarrassingly candid for our prurient predecessors. In 1819 King Francis of Naples declared that certain artefacts could be seen only by 'people of mature age and respected morals'.

Even today minors need to be accompanied by an adult – rather like an adult movie.

CASSANDRA: Pompeii's citizens will suffer the fate of the sinful men of Gomorrah!

LURCIO: Will they, indeed?

CASSANDRA: And Sodom.

LURCIO: Ooh, I agree, the lot of them!

From Up Pompeii *TV series (1971)*

STABILITY

The period from AD 96–180 became known as the era of the Five Good Emperors. Good emperor? Oxymoron?

— EMPEROR NERVA (AD 30–98) —

> 'No one would have doubted his ability to reign had he never been emperor.'
>
> *Tacitus*

Admit it, you've never heard of him.*

This senior citizen took over in a smooth succession from the deadly Domitian in AD 96. So smooth, in fact, there are suspicions he knew Domitian was about to be chopped.

He named Trajan his successor and then died after ruling a couple of years. This was a sensible decision and earned him the accolade of 'First of the Five Good Emperors'. That's a bit of an exaggeration. He simply wasn't strong

---

* You may say you've Nerva heard of him. If you did say that I couldn't possibly comment on your abysmal taste in puns.

enough to impose himself on the rebellious Romans.

He cared for the poor and the young and cut taxes. That nearly ruined the Roman economy and led to cuts in government spending. (Two thousand years later politicians are still struggling to square that particular circle.)

Overall, Nerva brought stability to the Empire and, best of all, he chose his heir wisely. Admittedly he was under a lot of pressure from the Praetorian Guard to choose the popular, young military man Trajan to follow him – the Praetorians were revolting.

Trajan made him a deity so he died a happy man. Nerva a better emperor.

BRIEF TIMELINE

AD 98 Trajan is made Emperor but it's over a year before he comes, to Rome. He's too busy plotting against Decebalus the Dacian. (That is roughly Romania today.)

AD 101 Trajan sets off on the Dacian War. Very popular with the Romans. After a tough year-long struggle Trajan wins through.

AD 113 After years of peace the Parthians are revolting and Trajan sweeps up large areas of the Middle East into the Empire. Too much. He hasn't the manpower to administer the new territories.

AD 117 Trajan sets off for Rome but has a stroke and dies before he arrives. The governor of Syria has been groomed to succeed but not adopted as the heir. A shaky start for Hadrian.

— TRAJAN (AD 53–117) —

> 'He prepares evil for himself who plots mischief for others.'
>
> *Latin proverb*

Plots, plots, plots … and Plotina.

Hard-fighting, hard-drinking Trajan had a soft spot. His wife Plotina was the power behind the throne. They had no children. Rumours of Trajan's preference for boys could explain that. But Plotina had a niece, Sabina. Plotina decided Sabina's husband, Hadrian, should be groomed as the next emperor. And what Plotina wants, Plotina gets.

It was never going to be a long-lived dynasty because Hadrian and Sabina had no children … Hadrian was attached to the youth Antonius.*

By the end of Trajan's reign the Roman Empire had never been so large and never would be again. His first problem was with the troublesome Dacians and their leader nick-named Decebalus 'Man with the strength of ten'.

---

* No you are not hearing an echo. Hadrian, like several before him, preferred boys. These emperors' penchants for boys were not so much a proclivity as a qualification.

Did you know ... Decebalus

Decebalus of the Dacians was a thorn in the side of the Romans for many years.

He began to needle the Romans with raids into their territory on the Danube. In AD 87 Domician set off to teach him a lesson and got a bloody nose ... metaphorically. Two legions were battered at a pass known as the Iron Gates. Like the Celts in Britain and the Cherusci in Germany, he was a master of guerrilla warfare – something the Romans always struggled to cope with. The Romans wanted set-piece battles and these barbarians refused to conform. How barbaric is that?

AD 88 Domitian's forces were defeated by the Dacians again.

AD 101–102 campaign Trajan finally forced Decebalus to accept Roman rule ... and all the while the Dacian leader was plotting to re-arm and strike back.

AD 105 Decebalus flattened a Roman force and obliged Trajan to conquer the country. Decebalus fled and cut his own throat. This charming vignette is captured on Trajan's column, erected by the emperor in Rome. It's still there, if you enjoy that sort of violence.

The Dacian's hand and head were removed as trophies. Decebalus would have preferred that to being led through Rome in chains and thrown from the Tarpeian Rock. Would you?

Trajan's long, painful conquest of the Dacians earned the Empire a fortune from the gold mines they took over.

Dacia ended up a success and its riches made the long

struggle worthwhile. It's harder to understand why Trajan had to charge off on a massive invasion of Parthia in AD 113. Another Jewish revolt drove Trajan into a fighting retreat. The Romans defeated Jewish revolts with the usual brutality.

Trajan died before he retreated all the way back to Rome.

Plotina announced that her husband had declared Hadrian should be his heir. But did Trajan *really* say that? Or did the wily woman wait till he'd turned up his toes before levering her niece into the empress's new clothes?

There is a suspicion that after Trajan died in a darkened sick room, the empress slipped a slave into his bed to croak, 'I name Hadrian as my successor … gurgle.'*

Was it all a cunning Plotina plot? We'll never know.

Where did Trajan's corpse end up? In a nice plot of course.

— HADRIAN (AD 76–138) —

'Gizza job! I can do that! I can build a wall!'
Yosser Hughes, character from Alan Bleasdale's
TV series Boys from the Blackstuff *(1982)*

The Roman Empire was getting fat. It waddled forward to take over some noisy, nuisance neighbour and always found there was yet another nuisance neighbour on its

---

* You'll have spotted the flaw in this conspiracy theory. If a slave took Trajan's place, then what did they do with the emperor's corpse while the impersonation took place? Stuff it under the bed? It all sounds very undignified.

doorstep. The Romans called them 'barbarians'.

The further the fat frontier expanded, the more nasty neighbours it acquired. The Roman Empire pushed out – the barbarians pushed back. Individually these barbarian bites and stings and needles and stabs were just small punctures on the bloated balloon of Roman expansion. Collectively they caused it to deflate.

Hadrian came along and decided to patch the borders, to stop the expansion, to consolidate. His answer was to build walls. Barbarians on the outside – Rome and its friendly provincial citizens on the inside. Even the mightiest wall, like Hadrian's Wall in the north of England, couldn't *really* keep out a determined enemy.*

Hadrian's Wall isn't simply a wall. It's a symbolic line in the sand. 'Cross it at your peril' was his message.

> 'Stay where you are until our backs are turned!
> ... He only says, "Good fences make good neighbours."'
> *From the poem 'Mending Wall' by Robert Frost*
> *(1874–1963)*

Hadrian's horrors

If Hadrian's grip on the throne was weak then he moved quickly to firm it up. He had four top generals executed for allegedly plotting against him. They were hunted down and killed. A trial was not considered necessary. Hadrian had put down a marker.

He set off to travel to almost every province of the

---

* The proof is that the Scots are still invading England to this day.

Empire. Quite an achievement. But his favourite spot was Greece – he wanted to make Athens the capital of Europe – and his favourite lover was the 14-year-old Greek boy Antinous. Hadrian even grew a beard because it was a Greek thing to do and many Romans adopted it as a new fashion. When Antinous drowned in the Nile in AD 130 Hadrian created a religious cult around his memory.

Hadrian fortified the provinces he could defend and forfeited the ones he couldn't. Pragmatic and, for a proven warrior, non-confrontational. A period of relative peace was descending.

When the emperor travelled through his provinces it was said he left a force of secret police behind to watch over Rome and seek out traitors.* His entourage was huge and put a bit of a strain on the places he visited.† Feeding the Hadrian hordes could lead to starvation for the peasants.

Hadrian's walls

Hadrian decided the Empire was as large as Rome could handle. Time to draw a line on the map and say, 'That's it.' And on the ground that frontier would be marked with physical signs – walls, fences or boundary stones. It wasn't a new idea.

Emperor Augustus had started a series of 'limes' – for-

---

* Walls have ears … so be careful what you say about their sausages.

† Elizabeth I of England inflicted herself on her rich citizens in the same way. She stayed with them till the food ran out and the cesspits ran over, then the circus moved on. The owners were frequently bankrupted by a Lizzie visit. The letter every lord in England must have dreaded was the one that began, 'We are pleased to announce we shall be honouring you with our company …'

tified borders in Germany with watchtowers along their length. They kept out the undefeated German tribes. These wooden palisades defined the boundaries in the north-west. But in that troublesome little island of Britannia the barbarians were revolting – again. Build some 'limes' to shut out the stirring Scots? No, there just weren't enough trees in the region. So Hadrian's Wall was built of stone. The legionaries laboured for six years to build this imposing wall.

To this day no one can agree as to why Hadrian expended so much effort to build something so imposing in a sparsely populated corner of the Empire and then used 9,000 soldiers to patrol it. Maybe it was a symbol of Roman oppression – like Norman castle or Christian cathedral. Maybe Hadrian was saying to the Scots . . .

> 'Look on my works, ye Mighty, and despair.'
> *From 'Ozymandias' by Percy Bysshe Shelley (1792–1822)*

Not many people know that Shelley wrote that poem in competition with his friend Horace Smith. Smith's poem was published a month after Shelley's and the final lines rather suit Hadrian's ruined wall today.

> 'What powerful but unrecorded race
> Once dwelt in that annihilated place.'
> *Horace Smith (1779–1849), English poet* ***

*** As Shelley got in first with the title 'Ozymandias', Horace had to come up with a new title. He came up with: 'On A Stupendous Leg of Granite, Discovered Standing by Itself in the Deserts of Egypt, with the Inscription Inserted Below'. Catchy eh? May explain why Shelley's poem is remembered and Smith's forgotten.

Hadrian's Wall also inspired a poem by W.H. Auden called 'Roman Wall Blues' that documents the misery of southern Europeans on the windswept northern Pennine ridge, guarding the wall.

> 'The rain comes pattering out of the sky,
> I'm a Wall soldier, I don't know why.'*
>
> *W.H. Auden, from 'Roman Wall Blues'*

Hadrian's policy wasn't popular back in Rome. An expanding Empire meant:

1 More jobs for the boys – the boys in the governing classes
2 More trade for the merchants with ever widening markets
3 More glory for the gung-ho lads in the army. Their motto was '*imperium sine fine*' – Power without end.

But Hadrian won through. A frontier was set and relative peace reigned – the *pax Romana*.†

Hadrian may have been a peace-making diplomat but he got it badly wrong with the Jewish rebels. He re-founded Jerusalem as a Roman city, Aelia Capitolana. His attempt to ban Jews from the city may have been a touch insensitive.

The last straw was Hadrian's tour of Judaea in AD 130

---

* It's either a badly written doggerel written by a semi-literate poet ... or it's a very clever poem pretending to be badly written by a semi-literate soldier. You decide.

† A term coined by Edward Gibbon in his famous book *The Decline and Fall of the Roman Empire*. He said the peace went on till AD 180. What happened then? Wait and see.

when he banned circumcision.* The new state knew a year of peace ... then a whole Roman legion was annihilated. That meant war. The Romans sent in almost half of the entire imperial army.

Simeon bar Kokhba led a Jewish revolt that went on for three years from AD 132 to 135. The cost to both sides was massive. The Romans employed a scorched-earth policy as they hadn't the forces to fight set-piece battles. The war cost the Judaeans 50 towns and 1,000 villages flattened.

The Romans ended massacring 580,000 in a Jewish last stand at Betar.

> 'The Romans went on killing until their horses were submerged in blood up to their nostrils. For seventeen years the Romans did not allow the Jews to bury their dead in Betar.'†
>
> *A Jerusalem chronicle*

Having built his frontier walls Hadrian died.

— ANTONINUS PIUS (AD 86–161) —

Antoninus was a peaceable bloke ... but that didn't stop him ordering other people to be aggressive on his behalf. So he sent his British commander, Quintus Lollius Urbi-

---

* No cheap jokes at this point please about Hadrian favouring circumcision because it was no skin off his nose.

† Yes, that is a long time to have corpses lying around. It must have been picnic time for the scavengers. In 351–352 CE, the Jews launched yet another revolt against Rome. Did the brutality at Betar work? Doesn't seem like it.

cus, to invade Scotland. Rather like the Grand Old Duke of York he marched his men up to the Central Lowlands and marched them down again.*

Antoninus was important because of what he *didn't* do … he didn't oppress the people on the other side of Hadrian's walls. He gave them time and peace to recover their strength. The strength to return to the attack refreshed. Meanwhile the Roman army turned soft.

He reigned longer than any emperor since Augustus. And if that is the most interesting fact about him he is a very boring man.

— MARCUS AURELIUS (AD 121–180) —

'Fortune-tellers of Rome should cover their faces or burst into laughter when they meet on the street.'
(They should be ashamed of their fraud or laugh at their own shamelessness.)

Cato (234–149 BC), Roman statesman and writer

Marcus Aurelius was a reluctant emperor. He assumed power in the spring of AD 161 but insisted Lucius share power with him. Rome had two emperors. A precedent for an east–west split. Was it the beginning of the end? Divided they fall? Not quite yet.

To reinforce his position as heir to Antoninus, Marcus was not only adopted by the old man – he married Anton-

---

* Unlike the Duke of York, Urbicus built a turf wall while he was up there. The Romans abandoned it. No one knows why. It took 12 years to build but the legions withdrew after 20 years, probably because it was attacked a lot more often than Hadrian's Wall.

inus's daughter.* She gave him 13 children – the unlucky
ones didn't survive their parents. Unluckiest of all were the
Roman people, because the son who DID survive was the
crack-brained Commodus.

BRIEF TIMELINE

AD 122 Hadrian sets off on a five-year tour of the Empire
and starts his wall across the north of England.

AD 135 The latest Jewish rebellion, led by Simon bar
Kokhba, is crushed with lots of blood spilt on both
sides.

AD 142 Now the Brigantes of northern Britain are
revolting. It could be that Hadrian's Wall had been
built to stop them uniting with allies in Scotland.

AD 162 Emperor Antoninus dies and the Parthians take
advantage of Roman uncertainty to rebel.

AD 165 The Empire and adjoining states are struck by
a plague. It could be measles or smallpox. It kills
co-emperor Lucius and the Roman defenders in
the Middle East are seriously weakened. Luckily
(for Rome) the German and Gaul enemy tribes are
weakened too. But in …

AD 166 … those northern tribes pour across the Danube
into Italy.

AD 168 The co-emperors make peace with the
invaders.

AD 177 Emperor Marcus Aurelius follows the school of Stoic
philosophy. The Stoics are no friends of the Christians

---

* Yes, that's right, he married his own sister. Their daughter was engaged
to co-emperor Lucius when she was aged 11. Lucius was her uncle. By
this stage of the Roman Empire, nothing of that nature should surprise
us.

so in this year, in Lyon, there are Christians tortured and thrown to the beasts. Vigilante mobs take the opportunity to stone and rape Christians. Marcus's son Commodus – a neurotic young man, not fit to rule a roost – becomes joint ruler.

As Marcus Aurelius's adoptive dad, Antoninus, had lain dying, the old man moaned on about the foreign rulers who had wronged him. One of these was Vologases IV of Parthia; he and Marcus were fated to fight. Marcus wanted to avenge the hurt done to Antoninus; Vologases wanted to throw off the control of Rome. He would test the strength of the new emperors and become a revolting Parthian.

In autumn 161 Governor Severianus led a legion into battle with the Parthians. A prophet, Alexander of Abonutichus, told him he'd win easily. He lost the war in three days, committed suicide and had his legion massacred. Not the best start to Marcus's reign.

Did you know ...

The prophet Alexander of Abonutichus was a conman ... a Gly-conman in fact. Awful Alex claimed to be a prophet and carried a snake named Glycon around with him. A cult grew around the god Glycon. But Glycon was in fact a glove puppet – a stuffed snake with a false human head.*

Alexander was consulted by Emperor Marcus regarding a Roman attack on the Marcomanni. Alex

---

* As his con worked we can assume the puppeteer was as pleased as Punch. That's the way to do it.

told the Romans to throw two live lions into the Tiber and a great victory would surely follow.* The Romans were smashed.

When challenged, Alexander said, 'Ah, yes, I said a great victory would follow. I didn't say WHO would be victorious.'

He made a fortune before dying of gangrene at the age of 70.

Co-emperor Lucius was given the job of restoring order in the Middle East. He dallied and debauched. Eventually he and his armies returned to Rome in triumph and brought with them an unwelcome friend – a plague. It could have been smallpox or measles.

> 'Louis Pasteur's theory of germs is ridiculous fiction.'
> *Pierre Pachet, Professor of Physiology at Toulouse, 1872*

The Romans turned to superstition, and the help of the gods, to combat the plague.

To us this may seem naïve – our prayers to win this week's National Lottery never seem to be answered. But from time to time a Roman prayer WAS answered. That gave the gods such a publicity boost that the superstitions persisted.

For example, Marcus Aurelius's armies were being battered in the Balkans. Emperor Marcus called on the gods for

---

* For those of a tender-hearted disposition you can rest easy … the lions simply swam across the river and survived. No report to the Rome Society for the Prevention of Cruelty to Animals is needed.

a thunderbolt to destroy the enemy siege engine – and that's what he got. A thunderstorm struck and saved the legion.

This plague would rage for 15 years and claim the lives of BOTH co-emperors. Lucius died at 39 in AD 169 and Marcus Aurelius in AD 180.

DANGEROUS DAYS DEATH VII

MEASLES

So how could measles kill so many people? After all it's just a spotty disease of children.

Measles is caused by a virus, part of a group of viruses called morbillivirus. This also includes dog distemper and cattle plague viruses. A nice little group of diseases.

It spreads very easily between people through droplets of spit and snot coughed and sneezed out. Nine out of ten Romans in contact with measles caught it, as they had not met measles before and had no immunity from the virus.

The first thing you'd notice is a bit of a stuffy nose and a cough – not so bad until a high temperature develops. Both eyes go red and it hurts to look into the light. Then a red-brown spotty rash appears.

Meanwhile the virus is busy doing real damage. In the lungs it is causing pneumonia, filling them up with fluid and pus. Unable to breathe, you become confused and lose consciousness due to lack of oxygen in the blood. Finally asphyxiation occurs and you die.

Measles not just a spotty rash but a real virus!

Dr Peter Fox

On the plus side, the plague also hit the barbarian tribes outside the Empire. The raids on the northern borders dwindled and Marcus was able to push that frontier forward again.

On the negative side the Empire was in the hands of Commodus – the first teen emperor since Nero – and look how *he* turned out.

When Edward Gibbon came to write his *History of the Decline and Fall of the Roman Empire* he dated it from the rule of Commodus. But he wasn't the first to claim that the rot started then. Even Roman historians spotted that Commodus was a turning point on the road to ruin.

> 'Our Roman history now descends from a kingdom of gold to one of iron and rust, as affairs did for the Romans of that day.'
>
> *Cassius Dio*

LIFE

— THE GLORY THAT WAS ROME ... IF YOU WERE RICH —

> 'Two nations; between whom there is no intercourse and no sympathy; who are as ignorant of each other's habits, thoughts, and feelings, as if they were dwellers in different zones, or inhabitants of different planets; who are formed by a different breeding, are fed by a different food, are ordered by different manners, and are not governed by the same laws: the *rich and the poor.*'
>
> *Benjamin Disraeli, from his novel* Sybil

Benjamin Disraeli was writing about Victorian Britain in the age of the Industrial Revolution. He could have been talking about Imperial Rome ... or most other eras, to be honest.

By the early 100s Rome was flourishing. The city was packed with public buildings. Of course the working classes who built, maintained and cleaned them wanted to live centrally. They crowded into the city along with the tradesmen, the snake-charmers, the jugglers and the acrobats. You all had to be central so you could walk to work ... there was no underground or bus service. The only way was up.

The tenement blocks rose, shakily, onto the skyline. Rapacious landlords built cheap and crammed in the tenants. (Not a lot changes there.) The higher you went, the more dangerous your life. Your gloomy room would be lit by candles or smoking oil lamps ... large windows would let in the light but let in the cold too. So you choked on the fug.

You'd cook on an open stove and no matter how careful you were there was always the danger a neighbour below would set the building alight. Your goose was cooked, and so were you. There was no fire escape and the cheap buildings burned like firelighters.

Did you know ... flying cows

It wasn't just fire that threatened you on the streets of Rome. Farm animals on their way to the markets could cause problems. A cow strayed down a residential street pursued by her owner. The panicking animal ran into the open door of a tenement and up the stairs. It kept going to the top and ended on the flat roof. There it slipped and fell into the street below, injuring several of the crowd who had come to rubber-neck.

The cow died.

— THE PLEBEIAN JOBS YOU MIGHT BE DOING —

If you had to live in Rome amid the workers then what job would you like? Some may be familiar on today's High Streets. Take your pick …

Hairdresser

A man walked into a hairdresser's. The hairdresser said, 'Lovely day, nice to see you, where are you going on your holidays? How would you like your hair cut?' The customer replied, 'In silence.'

Reputedly the oldest joke in the world

Modern hairdressers sometimes have to shampoo customers suffering from head lice. But that is nothing compared to what the coiffeurs and coiffeuses of the Roman Empire had to endure.

- To give your client a dark mane of hair, massage in liberal quantities of decomposed leeches.

- If the customer wants to be a blonde, mix pigeon dung with ashes. Rinse the hair in urine.

- Men who find shaving too painful may wish to have their face depilated. This can be achieved by applying bat's blood or powdered viper.*

---

* If you must try this at home please remember bats are a protected species now, so you could end up being barbered behind bars. And if you opt for powdered viper please do not lick your fingers afterwards.

Beautician

> 'Beauty, to me, is about being comfortable in your
> own skin. That, or a kick-ass red lipstick.'
>
> *Gwyneth Paltrow (1972—), US actress*

- If the lady wants a face mask, prepare one of Empress Poppaea's concoctions: mix breadcrumbs, scents, oils in honey and apply. Leave on overnight.* Wash off with ass's milk.

- For a face-powder the majority of women swear by white lead carbonate. Poisonous, gentlemen, but gorgeous so long as you don't want to kiss the lady on the cheek. A more exclusive and expensive foundation for the wealthy is made from white crocodile droppings. Again, kisses on the cheek are not recommended.

- A luscious lip colour can be achieved with a seaweed mixture, but the addition of vermillion will make the pout really vibrant. It is a toxic compound of mercury and poisonous, of course. She will look drop-dead gorgeous in her coffin.

- And if our beautician wants to add a hair-removal service for hirsute clients they can employ a specialist armpit-hair plucker as the Romans did in their baths.

---

* And hope there are no passing brown bears. Also hope you don't have the job of washing the pillowcases.

Dry cleaner

> 'All will come out in the washing.'
>
> *Miguel de Cervantes (1547–1616), Spanish author,*
>
> *from* Don Quixote

If you want clean clothes then take them to the cleaners. This was a job you wouldn't want to do yourself.

● The Germans had soap but the Romans stuck to the old ways to keep clothes clean ... 'fullers earth' (clay) kept fine materials like cotton free of grease. But tougher material like wool would be cleaned with a mixture of potash (plant ashes soaked in water) and urine.

● The cleaners would collect urine from public pee-pots placed on street corners. They were less keen on pub-toilet pee as its nitrogen content was too low. Those Roman cleaners knew their urine. They trampled the cloth in the urine mixture, often to live music because time pisses slowly.

> 'Gid Moaning, I was pissing by the door, at half pissed sox, when I heard two shats.'
>
> *Undercover policeman character in UK TV series* 'Allo, 'Allo

● Posh togas could be restored to a brilliant white by steaming them in sulphur. This also made them highly inflammable – like walking around dressed in the head of a match. Keep away from naked flames or end up as match of the day.

Fast-food outlet

There's nothing new about fast food. There were always tradesmen on the high street willing to sell a tasty treat or two.

- Appropriately the take-away pop-in shops were called *popinae*. Instead of a pizza outlet the Romans had *ofellae*, which was a cheesy dish.

- Where today we have a hot-dog stall the Romans had grilled sausages that could be sold wrapped in a sweet cheese bread. You may be less keen on delicacies such as the cooked lungs of goats or sheep.

- Fried chicken was available if you wanted it, but why not have a little variety in your protein and opt for stuffed thrush? A word of caution though. The thrush was stuffed without the insides being removed. Herring-gulls, ravens, jackdaws, swans, peacocks and coots and crows all had their own subtle flavour.* They'd be liberally sprinkled with a *garum* sauce, which was essentially the guts of fish, salted and left to rot in the sun.

---

* Romans in Britain ate storks too. Could you tell stork from mutton?

Did you know ... cook books

The writers of Roman food books believed in attention to detail.

Columella, writing in the 1st century AD, outlined the optimum breakfast to give slaves to get the best yield of grapes. He was following in the noble tradition of Cato the Elder (writing in the 2nd century BC), who helped the thrifty winemaker by calculating the amount of work a slave of the vineyard could do before dropping dead. So useful.

— THE POSH WAY TO DO THINGS —

If you could afford it then you had slaves to give you personal service. You also had a world of *cordon bleu* cookery at your table.

In the best-run households there was no waste, of course. So you would eat chopped udder of a sow as a delicacy rather than feed it to the dogs. Other joys of being rich?

- Sausages made from horse meat. (Make up your own jokes about mane courses etc.)

- Accompany your main course with a custard made with nettle leaves, a salad of dandelion leaves or stewed seaweed.

- The really rich, like Emperor Elagabalus (AD 203–222) enjoyed serving peas mixed with grains of gold and lentils scattered with precious stones.*

- A popular dinner-party delight was to disguise one sort of food as another – roast piglet was in fact made of pastry, eggs in a nest were pastry eggs filled with spiced garden-warbler flesh. (When the pie was opened those birds did not begin to sing.)

- Snails fattened on milk were popular, but if you were out to impress the boss, push the boat out and serve him with snails fatted in blood.

- Cute and cuddly dormice were fattened up on the best walnuts, acorns and chestnuts. A short life but a merry one. They were killed, stuffed with pork sausage and roasted. Dormouse consumption was considered a sign of status. In republican Rome a law tried to ban munching on mice – the law was ignored.

- The rich went in for quantity too. Emperor Maximian (250–310) ate up to 20 kilos of meat a day – a small sheep to you or me – and washed it down with 34 litres of wine.† Beer was a drink for barbarians. Some might argue it still is.

---

* The rich food clearly did him no good as he died at the age of 19.
† He was never going to be a poster-boy for the British Heart Foundation but he lived to see his 60th birthday … which is more than the dormice did.

Did you know ... wining women

Women were permitted to drink wine in the days of the Roman Empire. In the era of the Republic, bingeing babes had been banned. The poet Juvenal wrote in the 1st century AD:

'When she is drunk, what matters to the Goddess of Love? She cannot tell her groin from her head.'

A husband was legally permitted to kill or divorce his wife if she drank. One Roman legend tells of Egnatius Mecenius, who beat his wife to death with a stick for drinking wine. Another told of a woman sentenced to starve to death by her family. She didn't even get her lips around the bottle. All she did was open a purse containing the keys to the wine cellars.

The last recorded divorce for this offence was granted in 194 BC.

Some of the rich couldn't get enough food. They tickled their tonsils with a feather and vomited to make room for the next course.*

---

* There was a legend, perpetuated by school books, that the Roman mansions had a room near the dining room called the *vomitorium*. This was where they would have their Technicolor yawns. But that was a misreading of old plans. The word *vomitorium* simply indicated an 'exit' ... from the Latin verb *vomeo*, 'to spew forth'. Sick Romans like Julius Caesar went to the toilet to throw up, but on one occasion the great man went to lie down – smart move. Assassins had been waiting for him in the toilet.

SHAME

> 'Now this is not the end. It is not even the beginning of the end. But it is, perhaps, the end of the beginning.'
>
> *Winston Churchill*

— COMMODUS (AD 161–192) —

Then along came Emperor Commodus. For many historians his reign marked the beginning of the end. After the 'Five Good Emperors' you can guess Commodus must have represented the bad. He certainly had as bad a press as Nero.

His tutor was the famous Turkish physician Galen. But Commodus's great love wasn't learning, it was sport. He enjoyed taking part in horse racing, chariot racing, and fights with animals and men. It would never do for an emperor to be seen soiling his hands in the arena, so his fights were mainly in private. But he craved the applause – like Nero did for his singing – and eventually appeared in public – to the embarrassment of the senator classes.

Commodus reputedly ...

+ had 100 bears put in the arena, climbed onto a platform and from his safe vantage point fired spears and arrows till he'd killed them all

+ trained with the gladiators but he only fought with blunt weapons against feeble opponents

+ beheaded ostriches with sickle-headed arrows

+ killed five hippopotami in a day with his bare hands

+ executed criminals, who traditionally had stones to defend themselves – but not against the emperor

> 'He once got together all the men in the city who had lost their feet from disease or accident. He tied their knees together and gave them sponges to throw instead of stones. He killed them with blows from a club, pretending they were giants.'
>
> *Dio**

Fighting against Commodus was no laughing matter for the gladiators, especially the ones he used for practice. One gladiator fought against Commodus and both used wooden swords. The gladiator decided to flatter the emperor's skills and he fell to the ground, a beaten man. Commodus drew a REAL knife and stabbed the man to death.

Even when he wasn't trying to kill his partners he could still inflict damage …

** Dio thought the performance farcical. He forced himself to chew bitter laurel leaves to wipe the smile off his face as Commodus pranced about, proudly holding up the head of his victim … an ostrich. If Dio had laughed it could have been Dio's head having the panoramic view.

> 'When he was training, Commodus managed to kill a man now and then. He enjoyed making close swings at others as if trying to shave off a bit of their hair. But instead he often sliced off the noses of some, the ears of others and different parts of still others.'
>
> *Dio*

Commodus, who was a few brain cells short of a halfwit, started to think that he was the ancient god Hercules, returned to Earth. When he fought in the arena the senators were forced to attend and chant in unison like a soccer crowd, 'Commodus, Victorious, first among men …' and so on.

It must have felt wonderful for the vain young man.

> 'Is it not passing brave to be a King and ride in triumph through Persepolis?'
>
> *From* Tamburlaine the Great by *Christopher Marlowe*
> *(1564–93), English playwright*

Commodus was becoming a joke. An unhinged joke, capable of ordering the murder of anyone on a whim. Dangerous days for everyone in the Roman Empire.

Did you know ... Galen

Galen's father dreamed the god of medicine, Aesculapius, commanded him to send the boy to be a doctor.

He had a spell as doctor to the gladiator school of the high priest of Asia and cut the mortality for the wounded from sixty to just five. His wound-treatment was a cut above the rest.

Galen demonstrated his skills by slitting open a live monkey and inviting other doctors to replace the guts. They declined, Galen succeeded.

When he arrived in Rome he felt the doctors hated him and wanted to poison him.*

Galen helped the Roman armies in their wars against the Germanic tribes and was appointed court physician to Marcus Aurelius. When the Aurelian plague broke out he returned to Rome to help.

It was also known as 'the Plague of Galen' – not much of a compliment to a doctor.

Galen followed the wacky Ancient Greek theory of 'humorism' – that good health is a matter of getting your body fluids (humours) in balance. The four elements were blood/air, yellow-bile/fire, black-bile/earth and phlegm/water.

Medical students followed Galen's theories right up to the 1800s – and probably killed thousands. Patient sick? Too many fluids so let out some blood. Didn't work? Let out more blood. Dead? Oooops! Next patient please ...

Galen was appointed as doctor and tutor to young heir Commodus.

In AD 189 plague struck Rome again and 2,000 a day were dying. Galen clearly didn't have a cure.

---

* The term paranoia probably hadn't been coined then, but it seems he had it. Still he could have been the victim of a plot; just because you're paranoid doesn't mean they are not out to get you.

— THE CRIMES OF COMMODUS —

Uxoricide – wife murder

Commodus married Bruttia Crispina – beautiful but vain and haughty, they said. She seemed unable to produce an heir with him but in 182 she (probably) became pregnant. She was accused of adultery and exiled. Bruttia Crispina may also have been implicated with Commodus's favourite and most powerful freedman, Cleander. She had to go. She was around 18 years old.*

Eventually she was executed, though there is some dispute about exactly when. It was an arranged marriage and Commodus probably never liked her. So that's all right then.

Fratricide – sibling murder

Lucilla had been an empress before brother Commodus was an emperor. She'd married Lucius Verus when she was just 13. He died of plague. In AD 169 she was married off again, this time to Quintianus – a man twice her age. She wasn't happy and longed to be empress again. When Commodus became emperor she saw her chances of power fading.

In AD 181 there was a plot against Commodus led by senators. (He'd only been on the imperial throne two years

---

* Eighteen was around the age of Catherine Howard when Henry VIII sent her for the chop. Eighteen is a dangerous age for consorts. You are never too young to die … it just seems extra cruel to die so young and unnecessarily.

so they weren't giving him much of a chance to show how bad he could be.) One of the lead plotters was his sister, Lucilla, who reckoned her brother's nuttier-than-Nero instability would damage the Empire ... and she wasn't wrong there.

The assassination attempt was farcical. Lucilla and Quintianus's nephew used his status to get close to Commodus with a dagger. Instead of plunging it into the emperor and boasting afterwards he just HAD to announce his intentions first. The assassin brandished the knife and cried, 'See, this is what the senators are sending you!'

Commodus's guards reacted quicker than the sackless stabber.* He was executed.

Lucilla, sister or not, was exiled to Capri. Commodus later sent a centurion to finish off the rogue relative with a well-placed chop.

Homicide

Commodus took over in AD 180 but as a teen tyrant he needed help. He chose a brilliant slave, Cleander.

In AD 189, when famine struck and the Romans went hungry, Cleander proved his worth. A starved and angry mob marched on the palace; Commodus faced them with Cleander by his side. The bold emperor admitted the error

---

* John Wilkes Booth assassinated President Abraham Lincoln and he too had the urge to declaim about his actions. He shot Lincoln in the theatre box, jumped onto the stage and cried, a little like Commodus's assassin, 'Sic semper tyrannis' – 'See what happens to tyrants.' But Booth drew attention to his act AFTER he'd done the deed. A lesson to all would-be assassins. On the other hand he broke his leg when he landed on the stage which hampered his escape plans. Another lesson: kill, zip your lip, sneak out.

of his ways. 'I understand your anger,' he cried. 'Let me confess … it is all the fault of Cleander here.'

> 'Commodus lay dissolved in luxury, and alone unconscious of the civil rioting. Commodus started from his dream of pleasure and commanded that the head of Cleander should be thrown out to the people. The desired spectacle instantly appeased the tumult.'
>
> *Edward Gibbon,* The History of the Decline and
> Fall of the Roman Empire

The mob took the head and even avenged themselves on the son of Cleander. They went home happy. Hungry, still, but happy.*

Commodus somehow remained popular with the majority of the plebs. It could have had something to do with the lavish gladiatorial games he staged … and took part in. He paid by taxing the senator class.

Come-uppance-icide

> 'Then said Jesus unto him, "Put up again thy sword into his place: for all they that take the sword shall perish with the sword."'
>
> *King James Bible, Matthew 26:52*

---

* Please do NOT feel too sorry for Cleander. Commodus had a favourite called Saoterus whom he made chamberlain. When Saoterus the boyfriend was implicated in a plot against Commodus, it was Cleander who (a) murdered him then (b) took his top job. Dog eat dog – Cockapoodle Cleander eat Samoyed Saoterus.

Of course Commodus was going to perish as he lived.

Marcia was Commodus's favourite mistress. A little odd since she'd been part of his sister's plot to kill him in AD 182. She was probably a Christian and persuaded Commodus to go easy on the faithful.

Commodus saw himself as a gladiator and chose to celebrate New Year AD 192 with a parade from the gladiatorial barracks. Marcia and the Praetorian General tried to dissuade him – gladiators were low class and Commodus would look a right prawn … again. The emperor was furious at this lack of support and made a note to have the general executed – along with a few more senators to keep him company on the New Year's Day scaffold.

While Commodus had a bath his favourite boy found the list. To save the wax tablet from melting in the hot bathroom, he took it to Marcia. She saw her name at the top of the chopping list. She muttered …

> 'Oh, well done, Commodus. This is fine reward for the kindness and love I've given you, when all I had in return was drunken insults.* I have put up with you for all these years. A confused drunkard is not going to get the better of a sober woman.'
>
> *Marcia, quoted by Herodian (AD 170–240), Roman historian*

She gathered the other condemned men and decided to kill Commodus before he killed them. The Praetorian General

---

* 'All the kindness and love I've given you … conveniently forgetting I was part of Lucilla's plot to assassinate you, my darling.'

Laetus helped her.

Marcia, a consummate actor, took Commodus his wine as he stepped from the bath. It was laced with poison. The emperor's vomiting was so prolific they thought he'd expel the poison. So they bribed a young athlete, Narcissus, to strangle him.*

Commodus never even got to see the New Year in. Should auld acquaintance be forgot, for the sake of poisoned wine.

Did you know ... gladiators

Gladiator contests were similar to modern sporting contests in so many ways. Some things never change ...

1   Gladiators were the sports celebrities of their day and their closeness to death lent them a quasi-religious aura. The blood of a gladiator would cure epilepsy, the spear of a dead gladiator would bring luck to the newly-wed bride who parted her hair with it.

2   Gladiatorial contests evolved from religious ritual.† Blood sprinkled on a new grave brought blessings to the dead. At first humans were sacrificed‡ then later men were set to fight to the death over the grave. When the number of fights started to exceed three figures they became enter-

---

* Marcia was executed in AD 193 for her part in the murder of Commodus the year before. Finding that wax tablet had only delayed her execution by about a year. But given that she'd cheated death by escaping from Lucilla's AD 183 plot she'd had a good ten years. 'All they that take the sword etc.'

† Not a lot different from Olympic Games which were in honour of the gods of Mount Olympus. The sacrificial flame is still carried to wherever the games are held.

‡ Low-grade slaves usually, not expensive human flesh. Splash the blood, don't splash the cash.

tainments in their own right and were staged in arenas. The graveyard corpses were left to rot in peace.

3 In Republican times it was the custom to force prisoners of war to fight in their traditional uniforms and weapons. As the number of defeated nations increased so did the different types of gladiator. The staged combats featured gladiators fighting with swords and shields, spears and tridents, nets and daggers, helmets and varying armour. Romans were fascinated to see which of two contrasting styles would triumph ... they were international matches.

4 Though spectators are still at risk when they attend matches, the dangers are not quite on the same scale as those faced by Roman crowds. Emperor Domitian favoured murrmillo gladiators (short sword, rectangular shield, helmet) against Thracian gladiators (native spears and shield). An unfortunate spectator was heard to remark he preferred the Thracian to the emperor's choice. He was dragged from his seat and torn apart by a pack of wild dogs. Ruff justice?

5 By the days of the Empire gladiatorial combat was no free-for-all but fought to rules of combat. Like the Marquess of Queensberry Rules in boxing, the aim was to minimize serious injury. Gladiators cost their owners a lot to train and sustain so they wanted as many fights from them as possible. But ...

6 ... condemned criminals could be sent to die in combat ... and gladiators whom the crowd condemned to death were often still alive when dragged from the arena. They were in fact dispatched by a final hammer blow to the head from a backstage executioner. Claudius and Caligula courted unpopularity when they refused to spare popular but defeated gladiators.

7 Matches lasted 10 to 20 minutes, though the referee could

call for a time-out to allow the fighters to have refreshment and a rub-down. If a gladiator wanted to quit he would raise a finger in the air. Some contests ended in a draw and the referee made a decision. Like a boxing ref he could step between grappling fighters and give warnings. The top players were pampered with special diets – high-energy vegetarian usually.*

8 Gladiators were big business, like soccer today. There were top teams and star players who could make fortunes before retiring. But there was also money in merchandising. Hundreds of Roman artefacts – sculptures, figurines, lamps, glasses – depict gladiatorial fights. Even a baby's nursing bottle, found at Pompeii, was stamped with the figure of a gladiator. Perhaps the parents hoped the gladiator's strength and courage would be imbibed with the milk. You could get your very own gladiator action figure – David Beckham replica shirt anyone?

9 The similarity extended to rival sets of supporters fond of hooliganism. A contest between Pompeii and local derby rivals Nuceria led to riots and stone-throwing. Nero banned Pompeian gladiator contests for ten years as a result.

10 Today's soccer sees some coaches standing on the touchline screaming encouragement, advice or abuse. Gladiator trainers got very close to the action to bawl at their players. They were accompanied by slaves wielding leather straps that could be used to lash the reluctant or incompetent into action. This is something soccer coaches have yet to adopt.

---

* Research suggests this could have made the gladiators rather overweight in comparison to modern sportsmen and women. But if a man is holding a sword and a spear the average spectator is NOT going to shout at him, 'Who ate all the pies?' are they?

And if you want real evidence that human nature never changes, the Romans had *locarii*. What are they, you ask? The historian Martial wrote that Hermes was a super-star gladiator who always attracted more people than the arena could hold so he was good news for the *locarii*.

Have you guessed? Yes, they were ticket touts. Spivs in sandals.

> 'The Roman people desire only two things – bread and the games of the circus.'
>
> *Juvenal*

TURMOIL

— THE YEAR OF FIVE EMPERORS —

> 'Whoever wishes to foresee the future must consult the past; for human events ever resemble those of preceding times. This arises from the fact that they are produced by men who have ever been, and ever shall be, animated by the same passions, and thus they necessarily have the same results.'
>
> *Niccolò Machiavelli (1469–1527), Italian statesman,*
> *philosopher*

Maybe the Romans weren't paying attention in their history lessons. Their teachers must have spelled it out – 'Murder an emperor and you risk anarchy. Nero was driven to suicide and was followed by the Year of Four Emperors. We don't want that again, do we?'

'No, sir.'

Murder Commodus and there was no 'Year of Four Emperors'. There was a year of *Five* Emperors. It was a taste of the instability and in-fighting that would bring down the Empire. They should have invented revolving doors for them. They were …

— PERTINAX (126–193) LASTED THREE MONTHS —

Need to know … 67-year-old son of a slave. He spared Commodus's murderer – the Praetorian General Laetus – in order to win over the Guard.* He offered the Praetorians a cash bribe but was slow to pay. General Laetus prompted them to march on the palace. Pertinax had spared his life – big mistake.†

> 'Ingratitude's a weed of every clime,
> It thrives too fast at first, but fades in time.'
> *Sir Samuel Garth (1661–1719), English physician and poet*

The palace guards defected to the attacking Praetorians. Pertinax tried to reason with them. A soldier hacked him down.‡

---

* Easier said than done. Many of the guard wanted Senator Maternus. This wise man fled. He went so fast he left his clothes behind. Better the naked than the dead.

† Machiavelli said it is unwise for a ruler to be too kind and courteous and singled out Pertinax as an example. People like the Praetorians don't respect a considerate emperor and even despise kindness as weakness. Michael Caine had the same philosophy in the movie *Alfie*. 'If only fools are kind, Alfie / Then I guess it's wise to be cruel.' Michael Caine, an advocate of Machiavellian philosophy – not a lot of people know that.

‡ The soldiers responsible were later executed for killing Emperor Pertinax. As Pertinax was an unarmed 67-year-old man, trying to reason with his attackers, it is hard to shed tears for their fate.

— DIDIUS JULIANUS (137–193) – LASTED NINE WEEKS —

Need to know … The Praetorians wanted cash. (They usually did.) What better way than to auction off the emperor's position to the highest bidder?

Didius Julianus won.* He gave the treacherous Laetus the chop he deserved and then heard the bad news. There were THREE armies around the Empire who had each declared *their* general to be the next emperor. They were heading for Rome like some Monte Carlo rally with each one setting off from a different start line. Except it wasn't Monte Carlo but Rome … and the trophy would be Didius Julianus's head.

> *Mille viae ducunt homines per saecula Romam.*
> (Throughout the ages, a thousand roads lead to Rome.)
>
> Alan of Lille (1117–1203), French theologian and poet

Severus was the closest and got there first, swearing vengeance for Pertinax. The pesky Praetorians defected to Severus, the senate followed suit and condemned Julianus to death. Didius Julianus had never been popular, being booed and stoned whenever he appeared on the streets of Rome. He was killed in the palace by a soldier, just as predecessor Pertinax had been.

---

* If you fancy buying the title of Roman Emperor then the price in AD 193 was 25,000 sesterces to every man in the Praetorian Guard. The bad news is that doesn't guarantee you will live long enough to enjoy the power. In fact you could well have paid a lot of money for your own death warrant.

> 'Deserted, at his utmost need,
> By those his former bounty fed;
> On the bare earth exposed he lies,
> With not a friend to close his eyes.'
>
> *John Dryden (1631–1700), English poet and playwright*

The sad last words of Didius Julianus were, 'But what evil have I done? Whom have I killed?' Only yourself, Jules, only yourself. Stepping onto the throne is as healthy as swimming with piranhas.

— SEPTIMIUS SEVERUS (AD 193–211) —

Need to know ... When he entered Rome he was met by the Praetorians, who had declared for him. They expected to be rewarded. He dismissed them all and replaced them with his own supporters. He appeased the senate then turned his attention on the pretenders ... Pescennius Niger, commander in Syria, and Clodius Albinus in Britain.*

This was the man who had Perpetua the Christian and her friends thrown to the animals in Carthage. Dangerous days for pretenders and Christians alike.

---

* Albus = white; Niger = Black. So, like a chess match it was a contest between black and white. But it was an unusual sort of result because both black and white lost.

— PESCENNIUS NIGER (AD 140–194) —

Need to know ... Niger had a lot going for him when the powerful Roman armies of the East declared him emperor around the same time the armies in Germany were naming Severus. But Severus was ready for him. Niger's children were in Rome and were taken hostage. Severus marched east and defeated Niger's forces in a battle in Turkey. Niger was given the option to surrender and live in exile. He declined. He was defeated twice more and captured. No mercy now. He was beheaded.

Niger's head had an interesting journey. It was taken to Niger's base in Byzantium. This was meant to persuade the city to surrender. When the Byzantines resisted, Septimius destroyed the city. Niger's head eventually ended up in Rome where it was put on display. (A bit mouldy by then of course.)

And remember Niger's wife and children who were hostages in Rome? Severus no longer needed to kill them.

But he did. Not nice.

— CLODIUS ALBINUS (AD 193) —

Need to know ... Albinus had been sent to rule Britain.

He made a big mistake when he heard a report that Commodus was dead. He told his troops, 'Commodus was a tyrant. The senate should rule.' The senators were pleased. Commodus (who was not dead) was rather upset and recalled Clodius Albinus. For a man named White the future was looking black. Then a report came in that Commodus had been assassinated. We can imagine Albinus must have been a touch sceptical. But his life was saved.

When Pertinax was killed the British armies declared Albinus emperor. But Septimius Severus grabbed the throne first then cunningly declared Albinus could be joint ruler and the next emperor. Albinus may have been a little naïve to have believed this. After Septimius Severus defeated Pescennius Niger he changed his mind and set out to defeat Albinus.

First Severus sent a messenger with orders to assassinate his old pal. When that failed, Albinus crossed to Gaul. The two met at the massive Battle of Lugdunum (near modern-day Lyon). Some reports said there were 150,000 on each side.* Albinus was defeated and may have killed himself.

It's nice to respect a defeated enemy. But Septimius Severus, remember, was not a nice man. He had his dead enemy laid in the road so he could trample the corpse with his horse and chariot. Then he had Albinus's battered body beheaded and the head sent to Rome. The torso was thrown in the Rhone.

Of course Severus declared he would spare the wife and children of Albinus … just as he'd promised to spare the family of Niger. Again he broke his promise and had them beheaded. They joined Albinus in the Rhone.

Not nice at all. He didn't need to do that. It simply demonstrated he was afraid of the helpless.

> 'All cruelty springs from weakness.'
>
> *Seneca*

---

* Though sensible historians reckon the total was only 100,000. Still it was enough to let the battle rage for two days.

BRIEF TIMELINE

AD 180 It's back to the bad old days of evil emperors when Commodus takes the throne. He fantasizes he is Hercules reincarnated.

AD 192 The end of Commodus – murdered – and the start of the Year of Five Emperors. Severus and sons come out winners in the rat race.*

AD 208 Severus goes to York and takes sons Caracalla and Geta to give them a taste of imperial power.

AD 211 Caracalla takes over and quickly murders his brother to keep things simple. He will make all (freeborn) people within the Empire 'citizens' of Rome. A great honour which meant they could pay heavy taxes and be executed as citizens not barbarians. Christians rejoice.

AD 212 The German tribes are restless. Caracalla plans carefully and defeats them. They'll be back.

AD 218 Elagabalus – another emperor a few leaves short of a laurel wreath – takes the throne.

AD 230 The Empire is being attacked in the Middle East – Mesopotamia.

AD 238 The Year of Six Emperors and several litres of blood. There will be 49 emperors in the next 50 years. Sounds chaotic? It is.

---

* But, as they say, 'The trouble with the rat race is that, even if you win, you're still a rat.' With all that blood on their hands, Severus and his sons were hardly squeaky clean.

MISFITS

~ THE SAVAGE SEVERANS ~

'My father had a profound influence on me. He was a lunatic.'

Spike Milligan

Septimius Severus made a subtle change in the role of the emperor from 'first among equals' to 'divine lord' and all-powerful god. You can't argue with a god. His sons Caracalla and Geta were emperor elect and emperor-elect's-little-brother. They'd be trouble.

As usual it was the second-in-command who caused the problems. Plautianus was a trusted friend of Severus and became head of the Praetorian Guard. He made himself rich and powerful and married his daughter off to imperial heir Caracalla. That would have been a smart move, but Caracalla didn't much like his bride and distrusted Plautianus's power.

Caracalla said to Plautianus and his daughter, 'When I become emperor I'll kill you both.' The heir clearly had all the charm of his child-chopping father. Plautianus responded by plotting to eliminate the Severus family.* You can guess the rest? The plot was discovered and Plautianus executed.

Plautianus's daughter (Caracalla's wife) and his son were exiled. So did Caracalla carry out his threat to have his wife killed when he became emperor? Of course he did. She was strangled, along with Plautianus's son. Caracalla's daughter was in exile with his wife. He couldn't have his own child strangled, surely. But he did.

She was barely seven years old.

> 'Of all the animals, man is the only one that is cruel. He is the only one that inflicts pain for the pleasure of doing it. It is a trait that is not known to the higher animals.'
>
> *From 'The Lowest Animal' by Mark Twain (1835–1910),*
> *American novelist and humorist*

Like his Roman successor, Mussolini, Severus was forgiven his dictatorial ruthlessness because he was seen as efficient. Mussolini famously 'made the trains run on time'.† Severus campaigned in the East to defeat troublesome

---

* Known as getting your retaliation in first. Rome was such a dangerous place for people in power it was common to eliminate the opposition. The United Nations and the concept of negotiated compromise didn't appear to exist between Roman aristos any more than it did between Christians and lions.

† The train legend was pure propaganda. Many tourist trains were given priority on the rail network so the 1930s American tourists went home corroborating the myth of Mussolini's efficiency. The trains were no better under Mussolini than Mickey Mouse, but whenever a new rail bridge, or station or line was opened, Il Duce was there to take the plaudits.

tribes, rob rebel countries and enrich Rome.

Then he headed for Britain to bribe or batter the barbarians into submission. He based himself in York and left younger son Geta there as he marched north to survey the situation in Scotland and make a Pictish peace.

There is a story that Caracalla tried to murder his father on that journey. That was a waste of a sharp sword as Severus was already terminally ill. Maybe murder was his forte. He would go on to have his wife, brother, daughter and brother-in-law killed so why not his dear old dad? A full house in poker terms.

Severus returned to York and his deathbed. His advice to his sons (fathers everywhere take note) ...

1 Don't argue with one another, lads
2 Pay your armies promptly
3 Despise everyone else

As the evil eyes closed one last time you can almost hear the brothers mutter, 'Fat chance, old man.'

— CARACALLA (188–217) —

> 'God asked Cain "Where is Abel your brother?" Cain replied, "I know not: Am I my brother's keeper?" After this, God cursed Cain.'
>
> *Genesis 4:9*

Cain (the first human to be born) slew Abel (the first human to die). Abel was the younger brother of Cain, of course.

Geta was the younger brother of Caracalla. Maybe he

should have read the Bible for a little hint of what was in store for him. For Caracalla slew Geta ... or rather he had soldiers do the deed for him.

The brothers had returned to Rome where they divided the palace and blocked up any doorways connecting each half. On 25 December 211 Caracalla proposed a meeting; when his brother arrived he was greeted by soldiers who butchered him. Their mother had come to mediate the meeting. She ended up witnessing the fratricide. Geta died in their mother's arms – he was always her favourite.*

Caracalla held up his innocent (but blood-stained) hands claiming pre-emptive 'self-defence'. I had to kill him because he was plotting to kill me.

Caracalla set about exterminating all of Geta's supporters – some reports claim 12,000 died in the purge. The Greeks had a legendary monster, the Hydra. Every time a head was cut off two more grew in its place. Caracalla must have known that legend and should have learned the symbolism. For every single one of the 12,000 he killed there were families and friends who would vow revenge. In AD 215 in Alexandria he was met by a hostile mob chanting about his brother's murder. The emperor had these vocal critics massacred. But he couldn't kill everyone in the world.

Caracalla also set about erasing Geta's name on stone and papyrus inscriptions, destroying portraits. Geta became, in the term coined by George Orwell in his novel *1984*, an 'unperson'.†

---

* The poor woman was ordered to show no grief in public but to laugh and rejoice ... or her savage son would have her throat cut too.

† In modern times an unperson is written out of existing books, photographs, and articles so that no trace of their existence could be found in the historical record. Soviet leader Joseph Stalin revived the idea, even erasing people from photographs after their execution.

There were so many executions the senate were relieved when Macrinus, head of the Praetorian Guard, murdered Caracalla.

There was a rumour that Macrinus was prophesied to be next emperor. Macrinus said that made him a target for Caracalla so he had the emperor killed first. That's right … his excuse was pre-emptive self-defence. 'I had to kill him because he was plotting to kill me.' Sound familiar? Sometimes irony is sweet.

The man who delivered the fatal blow was Julius Martialis from Caracalla's own bodyguard. The emperor had had Martialis's brother executed a few days before on some spurious charge and Martialis was out for revenge. A dangerous man to have as a guard, one would imagine.

Emperor Caracalla stopped on a journey to have a pee in a ditch. The other guards turned away politely but the killer lunged forward and killed Caracalla with a single blow.* I believe the expression is 'caught with his pants down' is it not?

> 'Revenge is a kind of wild justice … vindictive persons live the life of witches; who, as they are mischievous, so end they infortunate.'
>
> *Sir Francis Bacon (1561–1626), English philosopher*

You can't say the infortunate Caracalla didn't deserve his fate. Macrinus took the throne. But not for long …

---

* Martialis must have been gloating and jubilant for at least five seconds. But even as he laughed till the tears ran down his legs, a Scythian archer of the Imperial Guard killed him. Swings and roundabouts old chap.

CRISIS

— ELAGABALUS (AD 203–222) – THE ODDEST EMPEROR —

> 'Who could tolerate an emperor who indulged in unnatural lusts of every kind, when not even a beast of this sort would be tolerated?'
>
> *From* Historia Augusta, *a Roman collection of biographies*

You may think you've met the most weird and wonderfully wacky emperors in history. But until you've met Elagabalus you ain't seen nothing yet.*

---

* 'You ain't seen nothing yet' is the first sentence ever spoken in a 'talkies' movie when sound swept in to kill off the silent movies. On 6 October 1927, actor/singer Al Jolson uttered those immortal lines. Elagabalus would not make a good subject for a movie – no one would believe his eccentricities. They just happen to be true.

Fact file – Elagabalus

- He came to power because Caracalla's aunt, Julia Maesa, didn't want to lose her imperial status. Emperor Macrinus had taken the throne but she started plotting to have her teenage grandson enthroned in his place.

- Elagabalus was priest to the sun god, Elagabal. The terrible teen looked a little like Caracalla so Julia told the Roman army in Syria he WAS in fact Caracalla's illegitimate son. They believed her and declared for the boy. When Macrinus marched to meet them he lost his nerve and ran away, disguised as a messenger. The soldiers caught up with him in time and lopped off his head. His son was executed too – not the first child to suffer for familial ties. Emperor Elagabalus was just 14.

- He maintained his love of sun worshipping, wearing priestly robes and leading dances around the altar. Romans were forced to worship at his statue – a giant phallus. Dozens of sheep and goats were slaughtered as sacrifices. Mixed with their sacrificial guts were said to be the guts of young boys – Elagabalus selected only those who had both parents still alive, so as to maximize the suffering when they were forced to watch their son's disembowelling.

- A lion, a monkey and a snake were locked in the temple of Elagab and fed on the genitals of his enemies. He said that all other Roman gods were inferior to Elagabal and he caused a massive scandal by parting from his wife (another Julia) to marry a Vestal Virgin (another Julia). His mother, yet another Julia, and his sister (you guessed it, yet another Julia) argued and caused chaos in the palace. He married Annia (not a Julia?) but first had to have her husband executed. Marital murder.

● One of his indiscretions was to invent an early form of whoopee cushion for guests at his banquets when they sat on the padded couches. A sort of wind in the pillows. A prank. But you ate well ... provided you liked camel heels, flamingo brains, tongues of nightingales or an amusing confection of severed parrot heads. Less amusing was his joke of releasing leopards and lions among the guests. Or the time he had two guests strapped to a water wheel and watched them slowly drown as it turned.*

● Elagabalus had his two male lovers elevated to positions of power. Not unusual. But when he began to wear heavy make-up and prostitute himself, standing naked in the palace doorway to lure in customers, the Romans were mortified.

● One historian reported, 'And even at Rome he did nothing but send out agents to search for those who had particularly large organs and bring them to the palace in order that he might enjoy their vigour.' Men were selected for high office according to the size of their manhood.†

● But he liked women too; he had a team of naked women harnessed to a chariot to pull him round his

---

* There is no record of whether it was still or sparkling water.
† He had baths built inside the palace so he could check out the men's privates.

gardens as he whipped them. And it seems he offered a fortune to any physician who could perform the surgery to give him female genitalia.*

● Elagabalus was generous to the plebs ... with a nasty twist or two. He'd give away lottery tickets at the games where you could win a slave or a house, if you were lucky. If you were unlucky you got a dead dog or a swarm of bees. On one occasion he threw poisonous snakes to the crowds with the lottery tickets, causing deaths by snake bites or trampling.

● Taxes rose to the dismay of everyone and senators were humiliated. Only his eunuch Gannys had the balls to tell Elagabalus to moderate his behaviour. The emperor was furious at the advice and stabbed him to death. Servants suffered. It's said he ordered a servant to gather a huge weight of cobwebs. When the slave returned empty-handed, he had him shut in a cage and eaten alive by dozens of starving rats.

● Granny Julia (the first one) persuaded Elagabalus to name his cousin as his heir. Elagabalus realized (rather late) that naming an heir was signing his own death warrant. Elagabalus and his mum went to the Praetorian camp to order his cousin's execution. Instead the Guards attacked the emperor.

● Historian Dio paints a dramatic picture: 'So he made an attempt to flee, and would have got away by being placed in a chest in a toilet, had he not been discovered and slain, at the age of 18. His mother, who

---

* They weren't up to the job. He made do with being circumcised instead. When they circumcised him, they threw away the wrong bit.

embraced him and clung tightly to him, perished with him; their heads were cut off and their bodies, after being stripped naked, were first dragged all over the city, and stuffed into a sewer.' The sewer was too narrow so his corpse was thrown into the Tiber. His granny Julia and sister Julia probably had a hand in the plot.* His friends were mutilated and impaled.

● Elagabalus's eccentricities were as sensational as those of Nero or Caligula. But it was his extravagance that would be his downfall. From palaces with urinals of onyx to gladiatorial sea battles fought on lakes of wine, he spent the money of the Roman citizenry and in the process devalued the currency. This was to have a damaging long-term effect on Rome.

> 'No fouler or filthier monster ever filled the imperial throne of Rome.'
>
> *Assonius (AD 310–395), Roman poet*

— 'THE MILITARY ANARCHY' (AD 235–284) —

> 'Rome shall *perish*; write that word
> In the blood that she has spilt.'
> *From 'Boadicea' by William Cowper (1731–1800), English poet*

---

* As usual you can find historians who will argue the original sources were lies and Elagabalus wasn't all that bad. That takes all the fun out of history, doesn't it?

To be fair, Mr Cowper, a lot of the blood she spilt was that of her own citizens … and her emperors contributed quite a few Roman bathfuls too.

AD 235–284 was an era in which the Roman Empire almost collapsed under the combined pressures of civil war, invasion, plague, and economic problems.

It all kicked off with the assassination of Emperor Alexander Severus by his own troops. In the next 50 years there would be around 20–25 claimants to the title of emperor – mostly army generals, usurping power over all or part of the Empire. There were more fragments of empire and emperors than you could shake a stick (or a sword) at. AD 238 was the Year of Six Emperors.

There were emperors in Gaul/Britannica to the northwest, Palymyrene (Middle East) to the east and the Roman Empire in the middle, while Spain briefly broke away too.

The senseless Severan emperors had each taken the throne by raising troops' pay till it was doubled and increasing the size of the army. How did they raise the money? Simple, they put less silver in the coinage.

But they didn't have the same grasp of economics 21st-century politicians have and inflation ran out of control.*

---

* Oh, all right, when I say today's politicians have a grasp of economics, we all know it is just about the level of a Roman emperor … or a Roman halfwit.

BRIEF TIMELINE –
THE ANARCHY YEARS

AD 217 The last Severan, Caracalla, dies, leaving the
Empire in financial trouble.

AD 220 Severus, aged 11, takes the throne with the help of
his mum.

AD 231 Severus invades Parthia but makes a hash of it.
The damage to his authority (and his mum's) is
terminal.

AD 235 The first of the barrack emperors.*

AD 243 Rome finally finds the stability to attack Persia and
wins. But they will soon be forced to a humiliating
peace settlement.

AD 250 The Christian persecution goes on as laws insist
Christians sacrifice to Roman gods. Meanwhile the
barbarians are coming: Franks and Alamanni cross
the Rhine.

AD 260 In the east, Roman armies are smashed at Edessa
(Turkey). Emperor Valerian is captured and killed.
Meanwhile in the west the governor of Gaul,
Postumus, declares an independent Gallic Empire.
Rome is too weak to prevent it, until …

AD 269 An invasion by a Goth army is thwarted at the
Battle of Naissus.

AD 270 Claudius II defeats the Alamanni but can't beat
the plague – that gets him.

AD 273 Rome recovers enough to crush the rebellion.
But the Franks are on the move, taking over
Belgium virtually unopposed. Frank meant 'free

---

* They would come and go faster and more forgettably than Chelsea FC
managers.

people'. The writing is on the wall ... and it's not in
Latin.

AD 280 In the Western Empire outlaw groups known as
Bagudae start to defy Roman rule. Some groups are
large enough to form armies, set up their own legal
and tax systems.

AD 286 Maximian in the west and Diocletian in the east
share the Empire. Carausius has been appointed
commander of the Roman forces in Gaul with a
brief to stamp out the Bagudae and Frankish pirates.
Instead he simply declares himself emperor of Britain
and Northern Gaul. 'I'm the third emperor now.
Get used to it.'

AD 297 Carausius is murdered by his successor Allectus,
who is in turn defeated and killed by a new Roman
invasion.

Peasants revolt

● The peasants took advantage of the anarchy to revolt.
Bagudae outlaws terrorized the Western Empire. If
the economy couldn't support them then they would
support themselves with robbery and piracy. Robbers
and pirates were not gentlemen of the roads and seas
– like Errol Flynn's fictional Robin Hood or his Captain Blood – they were cut-throats.

● They attacked the estates of the great landowners and
raided cities. Two Bagudae leaders, Amandus and
Aelian, were even proclaimed imperators – though
they probably weren't peasants themselves. The Bagudae were a motley crew with foot-soldier farmers,
cow-herd cavalrymen, the dishonourably discharged

and disillusioned deserters from the army. There were even reports of battling bishops.

- The Empire was also shaken by 'barrack' emperors … soldiers who led rebellion from within the army. There were about 14 of these legionary leaders in 33 years of the 'Military Anarchy'. They lasted an average of two years. None seemed to learn that as soon as they put their uniformed backsides on the throne they were doomed to be mayflies in the march of time.

- Some, like Philip the Arab (who ruled from 244), lasted long enough to make an impact. On the one hand he tried to tackle the financial problems of the Empire. Then he wasted a fortune by celebrating Rome's millennium in AD 248 with a spectacular slaughter of endangered species. A peace deal with Persia involved large payments too. Where did he find the money? He cut the subsidies paid to the tribes north of the Danube. They revolted.

- Then a familiar story. Decius was sent to suppress the rebels. He succeeded so well his troops said he should be emperor. They marched on Rome and killed Philip the Arab. In AD 250 an invading army of Goths did for Decius. The Sybilline oracle warned him …

'A blow will befall you from the arrow-shooting men. He will burn you and leave you entirely ruined and naked; anyone seeing you will break out weeping and you will be a prize of war.'

Not the sort of thing you want to read in today's horo-scope is it? In the words of Cassandra in the comedy sit-com *Up Pompeii*: 'Woe is us, and thrice woe, we are doomed, doomed.'

- Sure enough, in AD 251/252 three major cities were sacked, two armies destroyed and the emperor was powerless to turn things around.

- When Valerian took the throne in 253 he came up with the twin strategy of defending existing fron-tiers ... and actively persecuting the Christians inside those borders.

- Valerian was to claim the distinction of becoming the only Roman emperor to be held prisoner by enemy forces. When the Persians invaded he was used as a human foot-stool by his captor. He was then killed, either by having molten gold poured down his throat OR by being skinned alive. The skin was stuffed and displayed in a temple.*

- In the north a breakaway 'Empire of the Gauls' was proclaimed by Postumus and defended against Emperor Gallienus's attempts to crush it.

---

* But the historian was a Christian looking to describe a noble, martyr's death. Nasty story. Not to be trusted. Persian sources say he was employed as a navvy, building bridges.

DANGEROUS DAYS DEATH VIII

SKINNED ALIVE

In a ritual flaying the victim is tied by their hands and feet so that they're stretched out. A sharp knife is then used to separate the skin from the underlying tissues; mostly this would be done from the head downwards. Skin is full of sensory nerve endings, so it is excruciatingly painful. However although you may vomit and pass out with the pain it won't kill you. Death occurs from blood, fluid and heat loss.

Once the skin is removed the body starts to lose fluid and heat rapidly. You go into shock as the amount of blood circulating falls. With less blood circulating, the brain is starved of oxygen, you become confused, finally your heart stops. With no oxygen at all you die.

The good news is that most victims died before being 'half skinned'. The bad news is that flaying could be done very slowly – and to enhance the whole experience lemon juice could be squeezed onto the exposed underlying tissues. Tasty.

Dr Peter Fox

The Empire, assailed on all sides, was crumbling. Could anyone save it from the barrack emperors?

NEMESES

⏤ THE BRAVE BARBARIANS ⏤

> 'The mere notion of empire continuing to decline
> and fall for five centuries is ridiculous … this is one
> of the cases which prove that History is made not so
> much by heroes or natural forces as by historians.'
>
> J.C. Stobart, The Grandeur that was Rome *(1911)*
> *criticizing Gibbon's* Decline and Fall

From AD 235 there were to be 49 men proclaimed as
emperor, 25 of whom would be killed, 3 would commit suicide and one would be struck by lightning.* The Empire
didn't so much 'fall' as tear itself apart with power struggles. Plague played a part, as did a shrinking economy.†

But did the barbarian outsiders actively seek to sink the

---

* So first emperor Augustus maybe wasn't so daft for wearing protection
against lightning.

† In AD 270 Emperor Aurelian tried to improve the value of Roman
currency but even his coins were 20 parts bronze to one of silver. With
that lot in your purse you'd feel short-changed …

Roman Empire? Or did they merely see the Romans scuttling their own ship with feuds and infighting, and take command in order to preserve themselves?

And who were these barbarians? Would you feel comfortable in their company? Would you let your daughter marry one?*

— THE GERMANS —

> 'Wherever Germans are, it is unhealthy for Italians.'
>
> *Italian saying*

They didn't call themselves German, of course, but it's a handy historical label for the tribes of the area we now call north-west Germany. Their distinctive characteristics included …

- A man would not cut his hair or beard until he had killed another man in battle. By German standards, Santa Claus would have been viewed as a bit of a failure. But it didn't pay to be a coward …

> 'Deserters are hanged on trees; the coward or the unwarlike, is plunged into a bog with a hurdle put over him.'
>
> *Tacitus*

---

* The Christian writer Salvian suggested that the non-Roman peoples smelled rather badly. They didn't have the Roman way of bathing. On the plus side, they didn't go around crucifying people or throw them to packs of wild animals for fun.

- The warriors fought for their chief, not for some distant emperor they were unlikely to ever see. As a German warrior your performance in battle would be the stuff of legend in your family or tribe ... unless you screwed up and ran away ... or really screwed up and got yourself killed.

- A battle was a family affair with the chance of a picnic afterwards (or maybe at half-time). The women would encourage their warrior husbands with 'bosoms laid bare'.

> 'Close to the warriors are those dearest to them, so that they hear the shrieks of women, the cries of infants. The families are the most sacred witnesses of his bravery – they are his most generous applauders. The soldier brings his wounds to mother and wife, who shrink not from counting or even demanding them and who administer food and encouragement to the combatant.'**
>
> *Tacitus*

- They fought naked with only a shield to protect their body ... and their modesty. This was pretty off-putting for their Roman opponents who wouldn't know where to look. They certainly wouldn't know where to chop.

- They were a superstitious people ...

** 'Demanding' he accumulates wounds? Really? So a wife tells her husband, 'Get back in that battle and don't let me see you again till you've lost an arm or a leg – an ear at the very least.' Gives a whole new dimension to the vision of a nagging wife.

> 'They are addicted beyond all other nations to prophecies. Their method of divining is exceedingly simple. From a tree which bears fruit they cut a twig, and divide it into two small pieces. They throw them at random upon a white garment. Then the priest forms a judgement according to the marks before made.'
>
> *Tacitus**

● How will they know which way a battle is going to go? Have a one-to-one combat with an enemy …

> 'From the enemy they strive to gain a captive: they engage him in combat with one of their own, each armed after the manner of his country. According as the victory falls to this or to the other, gather a prediction of the whole.'
>
> *Tacitus*

● The dead German would be cremated. Onto the fire would go his weapons … and in some cases his horse. These same horses were denied battle armour because (Tacitus recorded) the Germans felt horse armour was 'unseemly and unmanly'. No one thought to ask the poor bloody horses. Not being men, they wouldn't have felt 'unmanly'.

Maybe one thing the Germans *weren't* was vindictive. When Arminius defeated the legions in Teutoburg Forest

---

* Given the Roman obsession with prophecies and oracles and omens, it's a bit rich to say the Germans were 'addicted'.

in AD 9 the Roman response was an attempted genocide of the Chatti tribe. Tacitus said, 'helpless women, children and old people were slaughtered or captured and their chief town destroyed.'

And the Romans called the Germans 'barbarian'?

— THE GAULS —

> 'A people in a state of revolution is invincible.'
>
> *Maximin Isnard (1755–1825), French revolutionary*

Living to the south and west of the Germanic tribes were the Gauls. The French – the revolting ones. They evolved from a branch of the Celtic people.

> 'Nearly all the Gauls are tall, fair and of a ruddy complexion: terrible from the sternness of their eyes, very quarrelsome, and of great pride and insolence. A whole troop of foreigners would not be able to withstand a single Gaul if he called his wife to his assistance who is usually very strong and with blue eyes.'
>
> *Ammianus Marcellinus (c. AD 330–91), Roman historian*

It was Julius Caesar who finally conquered them and they were largely assimilated into the Roman culture by the days of the Roman Empire. Historian Plutarch said the Romans had fought against 3 million Gauls, killing a million and enslaving a further million in the process. This is rather hard to believe. Certainly a Gallic leader would argue 1,800 years later …

> 'History is a set of lies agreed upon.'
>
> *Napoleon Bonaparte*

Gallic rebel leader Vercingetorix (82–46 BC) had tried to unite the tribes against the Roman occupation. His defeat was a highlight of the reign of Caesar. Conquering Gaul pretty much created a Roman Empire.

Vercingetorix didn't have the support of all the Gallic tribes. They weren't so keen to take on the Roman army and suffer the consequences. He led an army of beggars and outcasts. Of course they lost. But Vercingetorix was a showman ... even in defeat. According to Plutarch:

> 'Vercingetorix, who was the chief spring of all the war, putting his best armour on, and adorning his horse, rode out of the gates, and rode a circle around Caesar as he was sitting. The Gaul then quitted his horse, threw off his armour, and remained seated quietly at Caesar's feet until he was led away to be reserved for the triumph.'*
>
> *Plutarch (AD 46–120), Greek historian*

Caesar's own version of the surrender was that Vercingetorix was turned in by the other Gallic leaders, who were fed up with him. Whichever it was, he was the star of

---

* Vercingetorix is France's first national hero. A model for the French to follow ... if at first you don't succeed, surrender. Celtic tradition demanded that a warrior should kill his family and then kill himself rather than see them all taken into slavery. Vercingetorix decided to take the white-flag alternative.

Caesar's 'triumph' – a parade in Rome to honour Caesar's victory.

The grand finale of the triumph was the execution of Vercingetorix. He made his final show, dragged behind Caesar's chariot through the streets of Rome … but probably did not die singing, *'Je ne regrette rien'*. It's hard to sing when you are being strangled (though some may argue there are pop stars today who give a good impression of this feat).

The Romans may be credited with creating modern society. But it was the Gauls who created the feudal system that still oppresses many countries (like Britain) today … You know the feudal pyramid from your school textbook illustrations: a king at the top who owns the land, lords and priests below who get a share in exchange for their support, and peasants at the bottom who do the real work … even though we are the majority. Thanks Gaul.

The only time Gaul broke free in the days of the Roman Empire was around AD 260. Rebel general Postumus (a German by birth) declared himself emperor of a break-away Gallic nation. He refused to let his soldiers loot a conquered city so, naturally, they murdered him.

– THE CELTS –

'The Welsh are not like any other people in Britain, and they know how separate they are. They are the Celts, the tough little wine-dark race who were the original possessors of the island, who never mixed with the invaders coming later from the east, but were slowly driven into the western mountains.'

Laurie Lee (1914–97), British poet and novelist

The Celt tribes of Britain have had a bad press. That is mainly due to the fact the reporters were Greek or Roman. They made the Celts into monsters.

'The Celts are terrifying in appearance with deep-sounding and very harsh voices. They use few words and speak in riddles. They often exaggerate with the aim of making themselves look good and making others look weak. They are boasters and threateners, yet they have quick minds and a natural ability for learning.'

Diodorus Siculus, 1st Century BC

Diodorus Siculus was Greek and not up for a fight. But despite being a fellow Greek, the geographer Strabo was a little more dismissive of the Celt warriors.

'I myself, in Rome, saw boys a head taller than the tallest Roman. But they were bow-legged and showed no fine features. Their power lay in their vast numbers.'

Strabo (63 BC–AD 24)

So they were as tall and bandy as John Wayne, and as ugly and numerous as Bilbo Baggin's Orc enemies.

According to the Romans the brutal Celtic Brits …

◆ believed they could gain a defeated enemy's strength and wisdom by cutting off his head

◆ liked to keep enemy heads as trophies, and would preserve them in cedar oil, displaying them on their walls or around their doors

✦ believed their Druid priests had magical powers such as shape-changing, controlling the weather, bringing down mists to make themselves invisible and travelling through time

✦ would pacify their gods with human sacrifices – often 'death by air' i.e. suffocation, strangulation or hanging*

✦ fought naked and painted themselves with blue dye known as woad, wearing only a golden torque around their necks

✦ would slaughter their own families to save them from slavery if they were losing a battle

✦ upon invading a country and marrying its women, the warriors cut out the tongues of their brides so the pure language of the men would not be spoiled by the foreign language of the wives†

✦ were inveterate binge drinkers and took part in contests to brag about their fighting exploits

― THE DACIANS ―

The genocide of the Chatti tribe was small scale in comparison to the extermination of the Dacians. To rub salt into the memory of Dacia it was even renamed for Rome … we call it Romania.

---

* Roman outrage at Druid human slaughter is a bit rich, given the way the Romans killed people on an industrial scale. Pot. Kettle. Black.
† Almost certainly apocryphal.

- In AD 106 Emperor Trajan set out to destroy his noisy neighbours. His doctor, Criton, gloated that when Trajan had finished with them there were just 40 Dacians surviving. Trajan himself thought it worthy of a boast ...

> 'I have single-handedly defeated the people from the far side of the Danube. I have annihilated the people of Dacia.'
>
> *Emperor Trajan*

- The claim that only 40 were left is certainly a boast too far, but Dacia was drained of its population as the natives were taken as slaves or as soldiers in Roman legions. So the people weren't 'annihilated' ... but their culture, their traditions and their religion seem to have been.

- Unlike the German tribes, the Dacians were rich 'beyond the dreams of avarice' – a phrase probably coined by English playwright Edward Moore (1712– 57). When Dacia was looted by Rome, the armies brought home over 1,500 tons of gold and over 3,000 tons of silver.

- If Rome was 'civilized' with their paved roads, literate lords, stone buildings, classical statues, sophisticated plumbing, artistic pottery, finest metalwork and a powerful religious ethos, then Dacia was at least as good as Rome. It just wasn't so aggressive or ruthless until ...

- Decebalus took over as Dacian ruler, and in AD 85 crossed the Danube and killed the Roman governor.

Emperor Domitian had to respond, so Decebalus was forced to be a client king to Rome – a token gesture, as far as he was concerned. But when Emperor Trajan took over, nothing would satisfy the Romans but total domination.* By AD 105 Rome had triumphed: Decebalus killed himself. Time to head off to Rome for his head.

● The Romans worked the gold- and silver-mine slaves to death – literally. Bodies of Dacian slave workers were stacked in heaps when they pegged out. So much gold was sent to Rome the bottom fell out of the gold market. How those mining slaves must have laughed. But the legacy of devastated Dacia was to spell the end for Rome. It had no defensible borders so instead of being a buffer against the barbarians to the east it was an open door. Come this way, lads, if you want to overrun Rome.

● Dacia was all but erased from history. Yet still the proud name 'Dacia' lives on … in a car brand advertised as 'Shockingly affordable'. It is made in Romania (where else?) and has models with catchy names like Duster. Maybe named for Trajan: the Dacia Duster … the man who polished off Dacia?

> 'The song is ended, but the melody lingers on.'
> *Irving Berlin (1888–1989), American composer and lyricist*

---

* Decebalus also tried to organize the assassination of Trajan through some disaffected Roman soldiers. One was caught and tortured and betrayed the plot. Trajan, unamused, hardened in his determination to crush Dacia. You would, wouldn't you?

DECLINE

> 'Almost all barbarians, at least those who are of one race and kin, love each other, while the Romans persecute each other. Nay, the state has fallen upon such evil days that a man cannot be safe unless he is wicked.'
>
> *Salvian (born AD 400), Christian writer*

~ THE DOMINATE ERA ~

Barrack emperors passed the parcel of emperorship as if it contained a ticking bomb. The instability threatened ruin. Yet it was ex-soldiers who finally brought third-century anarchy to an end. Aurelian (AD 215–275) defended Italy desperately and won through, despite losing a major battle and having to deal with a revolt in Rome. He finally swept the enemies out. He was assassinated – par for the course.

Did you know …

… the death of Aurelian was rather an unusual one. Aurelian's Secretary, Eros, told a little lie and was then terrified that the strict Aurelian would punish him severely. So Eros forged a document purporting to show officials marked down for execution by the emperor. He showed it to them and they pre-empted their own execution by butchering Aurelian.

Aurelian's short reign had stopped the rot. The army in the East elected their general Probus, who met with Aurelian's assassins to discuss 'reconciliation' over dinner. Imagine you were one of the assassins who'd murdered the emperor. Would you accept?

They did. They died. Assassinated.

Didn't they read their history books? Dispute resolved. Probus rules … until he is assassinated by disgruntled soldiers.*

Did you know …
something rotten in the state of Rome

One of the barrack emperors, Numerian, died in AD 284 as he was travelling by coach. Some of Numerian's soldiers smelled the decaying corpse. They opened its

---

* One story says it was a bit of an old trades union demarcation dispute … the soldiers were employed to fight, Probus wanted them to do civil works like drain mosquito-infested marshland. They drained his blood instead. Easier.

curtains and found Numerian dead. But the killers couldn't decide on a replacement. To announce his death without a successor lined up would invite chaos. So they made his apologies – 'He has an eye infection. Can't make public appearances' – and let him remain in his litter till the smell of his rotting body gave the game away.

The cavalry commander, Diocletian (AD 244–311) took control in AD 285. He was raised on a platform and proclaimed emperor by Numerian's minister, Flavius Aper. Diocletian raised his sword to accept the acclamation … then turned it on Flavius Aper, accused him of assassinating Numerian and cut him in two. (Freud would probably have diagnosed him as a split personality.)

Diocletian proved a stabilizing emperor. He introduced a system of emperors called the Tetrarchy – four rulers, two emperors and two juniors known as 'Caesars' – and completed Aurelian's job of restoring stability.

After 20 years Diocletian retired … to grow cabbages. When asked to resume power a couple of years later he said …

> 'If only you could see the vegetables I have grown by my own hand you would never dream of asking such a thing.'

Want an imperial throne? No thanks, I'd rather have a carrot.

'Barrack' emperors came to be replaced by 'shadow' emperors like Stilicho, military bully boys who effectively ruled the Empire as generalissimos while puppet emperors held the title in name only.

> 'For ten years Caesar ruled with an iron hand. Then with a wooden foot, and finally with a piece of string.'
>
> *Spike Milligan*

At least it brought to an end the anarchy that had threatened to make the Empire implode.

The death of the Empire was deferred.

— THE END IS NEAR ... —

If the Roman Empire was disintegrating, there weren't a lot of people willing to patch it up. With so many cruel emperors and so many cruel practices, Roman rule was heartily detested. Even the provinces who didn't actively take up arms against Rome were quite happy to watch it sink and drown in its own cesspit.

Then it was the turn of the Christians to do their worst. In 306 the legions in Britain proclaimed their own emperor (again). This time it was Constantine, who would go on to conquer Rome and take over the Empire. And he became a Christian in 312. The persecuted little sect had risen to rule the world. Matthew would have been pleased to see his prediction come to pass:

> 'So the last shall be first, and the first last.'
>
> *Matthew 20:16*

Constantine apparently had a vision before a crucial battle against rival Maxentius: 'Fight under the symbol of the Christian cross and you will win.' He did and he won. Max, follower of the sun god, lost. Maybe the sun god was upset with the loser because as Maxentius fled he drowned in the Tiber. Constantine became all-powerful. Max, like an overspent credit card, was Maxed out.

Did you know ... Maxentius

After Max's drowning, Constantine portrayed him as an enemy of Christians and a tyrant. Historians believed him, until very recently. Constantine claimed credit for building the great Basilica in the Roman forum – in fact it was Max's achievement.

Constantine fell out with son-and-heir Crispus and had him executed. It might have been because his wife, Fausta, accused her step-son of attempted rape. (That would make way for her own sons to inherit.) After Crispus was dead, Constantine discovered the truth and had Fausta killed; she was suffocated in an over-heated bath.*

Not very 'Christian' acts ... considering you're a Christian hero, Constantine.

Constantine died in AD 337 and for the next 150 years the Western Empire would be governed from Constantinople.

---

* Another theory is mother and step-son really did have an illicit affair. Crispus was executed at once. Fausta had to wait as she was pregnant at the time. You pays your money, you takes your choice.

'Rome is the only monument left of Rome,
And only Rome vanquished Rome.'

Joachim du Bellay (1522–60), French poet

After the death of Constantine the downhill slope got steeper and more slippery ... probably with blood.

The Romans were heavily defeated in Persia in AD 363 and Emperor Valens took over. By the time Alaric the Hun was born in AD 370, the Huns from the east were arriving and driving the Goths across the Danube into Roman territory. Emperor Valens allowed these western Goths (or Visigoths) in, so long as they were unarmed and the pagans among them converted to Christianity.

As usual it was Roman greed and arrogance that caused trouble. The Goths in their refugee camps were promised food by the emperor. But the middle-management withheld it in order to profiteer. They wanted slaves from the Visigoths and would hand over dead dogs as meat in exchange – one slave earned you one dead dog.

The Visigoths revolted – wouldn't you? Emperor Valens led the Roman army against them and at Adrianople in AD 378 he was killed.

Under the leadership of young Alaric, the Visigoths revolted again in AD 395 and rampaged through the Eastern Roman Empire, slaughtering men, women and children in the cities they pillaged. Then in AD 401 they headed west ... towards Italy.

BRIEF TIMELINE ...
4TH CENTURY

AD 303 The last great persecution of the Christians begins.

AD 312 Christian Constantine defeats rival emperor
Maxentius in a battle near Rome.

AD 324 Con goes on to defeat Eastern Emperor Licinius
and rule the Empire. He develops Byzantium to
be the new capital and has it named after him ...
Constantinople.

AD 337 Crucifixion banned but equally pleasant
executions replace it. Anyone for molten lead poured
down the throat?

AD 353 Constantius II defeats Western usurper to rule
alone. For eight years.

AD 360 Public disorder in colonies like Britain.
Disaffection with Roman rule is bubbling along like
a pressure cooker.

AD 363 Heavy defeat in Persia shakes the Empire. Ten
years later the Goths are driven into Roman territory
by Huns migrating from the east.

AD 368 Picts from Scotland and Franks attack Britannia.
It's haggis and snails for tea then.

AD 376 The Huns drive the Goths and Alans into Roman
territory. The start of the 'Barbarian Invasion' which
will last 220 years.

AD 378 Roman treatment of the Goths causes them to
rebel. They kill Emperor Valens at the battle of
Adrianople.

AD 391 Emperor Theodosius says Christianity is the
ONLY religion that will be tolerated. The wheel of
fate has turned.

AD 394 It's a showdown between the old gods and the new.
A Frankish general (old gods) is defeated by devout
Christian Theodosius. Theo said God was on his
side. They all say that.*

---

* The Christians were helped in battle by a sudden and violent storm.
St Matthew's gospel proclaimed 'God blew and they were scattered'. That
was to become the motto of the English after the defeat of the Armada in
1588. God did a lot of blowing and scattering through history. Sadly He
didn't do any appearing and saying, 'Come on, lads, let's sit down and talk
about this.' That would take far less heavenly breath.

FALL

Roman historians blamed the Empire's collapse on moral decline – greed and luxurious living made them soft. Modern historians have more fanciful theories … they declare, 'The Romans died of lead poisoning from their water pipes.'*

Others say the Christian religion was to blame. Certainly by AD 390 it was ruling the roost. Theodosius ordered a massacre in the province of Thessalonica to teach the rebels a lesson. The Bishop of Milan made the emperor do public penance. An emperor saying 'Sorry for killing people'? (He didn't say it to the heaps of dead, of course.)

Some historians have even argued that the Roman Empire didn't fall at all. So why is no one chatting in Latin today? Most agree the Empire disintegrated and barbarian invasions played a part.

---

* There is as much evidence of lead poisoning as for the theory the barbarians were assisted by aliens in flying saucers.

— THE VISIGOTHS —

> 'A race of men, unknown till then, had arisen from some corner of the earth. Like a storm of snow from a high mountain this race was grasping and destroying everything in its path.'*
>
> *Ammianus Marcellinus*

Think of 'the decline and fall of the Roman Empire' and you think of the famous sack of the city by Alaric the Goth in AD 410 … Except it wasn't that simple. The Goths weren't a heathen mob, they were Christians. And Alaric had been a Roman general before his oppressed people needed his help to find a new homeland. So what is the truth about the Goths?

- By AD 250 the Romans had effectively deserted Dacia. Nature abhors a vacuum and the Goths began to move in. The Romans resisted, but in the end Emperor Aurelian re-drew the border to the Danube where it had been in the early imperial days.

- A hundred years later and the Huns from the east were driving the Goths west, across the Danube into Roman territory. In their desperation to escape, some refugees tried to swim the Danube and drowned. Roman observers lost count of the tens of thousands

---

* Nobody comes from nowhere. The Huns probably originated in the Asian Steppes or Siberia. As Siberia is a byword for punishing climate you can understand why they fancied mugging the Visigoths for their land.

of fleeing Visigoths.*

- The Visigoths were Christians and fighting for the Christian emperor Theodosius in the east. After years of persecuting Christians the tide was flowing very much the Christian way. But why did Theodosius put the Visigoths in the front line? They 'won' but Theodosius claimed they lost 10,000 men. Theodosius boasted he'd craftily beaten his Western rival AND weakened the Visigoths.†

- Alaric became the Visigoth leader. He was young but wise, a great warrior, a clever planner, ruthless when he had to be, but cared deeply for his people. Apart from the 'ruthless' bit he would never make a Roman emperor. But it was Alaric who would be the earthquake to shake Rome to its foundations. He marched his Visigoths into Italy.

- The skilful General Stilicho defeated Alaric and his Visigoths‡ near Turin in 402. But Alaric escaped with most of his army. The following summer he was defeated again. But Alaric was useful to Stilicho for his own ambitions and they made a peace pact. The Visigoths were paid off and the Empire was saved … for a little while. Some 30,000 Visigoth warriors joined Stilicho's army.

---

* But I can tell you one Roman said there were as many refugees as there are 'grains of sand on the Libyan plain'. So go to Libya, count the grains and you'll have your answer.

† Which just goes to prove that emperors, as well as historians, were capable of fibbing. There were only 10,000 Goths in the Goth attack.

‡ The Visigoths cried 'Foul!' – Stilicho had attacked on Easter Sunday 402 when Alaric's Visigoths were all at prayer.

They'd be back.

— HOPELESS HONORIUS —

In AD 407 Honorius (384–423), the halfwit young emperor, was suspicious that his great general Stilicho had designs on the imperial throne. So what did he do? He had Stilicho executed, of course.* It was another nail in the Roman Empire's coffin. If you've killed your best general in the fight against the barbarians then no emperor in his right mind would provoke the barbarians into a fresh attack. Rome had an emperor who was clearly not in his right mind.

Did you know ... Honorius

Born in AD 384, Honorius was a consul at the age of two. A nappy start to his rise to power.

AD 395 He became Western Emperor at the age of ten but would never have passed an 11+.

There is a story that he had a beloved pet chicken he called 'Rome'. When Alaric the Visigoth attacked the city, a messenger brought news: 'Rome has perished!' Honorius was truly distressed ... till he realized they were talking of the city, not the hen.

His other claim to fame – or infamy – was that he passed a law banning men from wearing trousers in Rome.†

---

* In keeping with the traditions of imperial sneakiness, Stilicho was tricked into surrendering. He was in the sanctuary of a church when officers arrived to arrest him. 'We're only here to take you into custody. We aren't here to execute you.' He believed them. They executed him.
† Barbarians wore trousers. They still do.

AD 408 Emperor Honorius incited the Roman citizens to exterminate the Visigoths' wives and children in Rome – the families of Stilicho's Visigoth legions. Naturally those 30,000 furious Visigoth soldiers joined Alaric's rebels and targeted Rome to avenge their murdered families.

AD 407 Honorius was caught cold when the Rhine froze and the barbarian hordes were able to walk across the usually formidable barrier. Hard luck, Honorius.

When the Visigoths moved to Italy in AD 408 Honorius shifted his capital to Ravenna, where the marshes made a natural defensive barrier.

AD 408 He had his father-in-law, General Stilicho, executed but needlessly had his mother-in-law executed too. It left Rome without a brilliant general. Yet Honorius survived the Visigoth takeover in 410.

AD 417 He married his sister off to his capable commander Constantius. She did NOT want to marry him. Luckily Constantius died in 422.

By the time Honorius died in 423, Rome had lost Britain, Spain and Gaul to the barbarians.

– AWESOME ALARIC –

> 'When you have to kill a man, it costs nothing to be polite.'
>
> *Winston Churchill*

In AD 410 Alaric and the Visigoths marched on Rome and besieged it. Food ran so low there were reports of terrible atrocities inside the city.

> 'The citizens of Rome were in great danger of being eaten by each other. There were reports of a mother eating her new-born child.'
>
> *Zosimus (490s–510s), Byzantine historian*

The Romans capitulated, paid Alaric in gold and spices and released barbarian slaves. Alaric sent peace terms to Honorius. They were reasonable terms. Honorius rejected them on the reasonable grounds that he was an idiot.

Alaric marched into Rome and took over.

◆ There was little violence and only a few small fires.

◆ Sanctuary in holy places was respected by the invaders.

◆ Religious gold- and silver-ware went untouched.

◆ The emperor's sister, like the Roman women, was spared being ravished.

> 'The bright light of the world was put out; the whole world perished in one city.'
>
> *Saint Jerome (347–420), Christian historian*

Saint Jerome started the myth that Alaric's sack of Rome was a world disaster. It wasn't. The city wasn't that critical to the survival of the Empire. Honorius continued to rule from Ravenna and the Empire of the East was strong in Constantinople.

As spectacular displays of pyrotechnics go, the 'sack' was not quite a *damp* squib, but it was certainly a very *small* one. Still, it was enough. Like a puff of wind to a house of cards it was a blow that marked the start of the final decline of the Empire.

But in AD 410 Honorius still controlled Africa, the grain supplier of Rome. Alaric had to march to Carthage to control those supplies. He died on the journey. Who knows how great a leader he could have been. He certainly provided the spark that lit the Visigoth fires.

The Romans continued to self-destruct. After Honorius died in AD 423 the Western throne was snatched by a soldier's choice, John. The Eastern Emperor, Theodosius, sent an army to capture him. John sent for a massive force of Huns to help his cause. The race was won by Theodosius's army. John was captured, paraded in an arena mounted on an ass with one hand cut off, then tortured before being put to death.

The 'games' may have ended with the coming of the Christian emperors – the Roman love of human suffering hadn't. It's odd that the most brutal feature of Roman life had been the cruelty of the 'games'. Honorius oversaw the last 'games' and he also saw the Empire slide towards ruin.

Did the Romans need their cruelties to survive?

— THE HUNS AND AWFUL ATTILA —

'History is a nightmare from which we are trying to awaken.'

James Joyce (1882–1941), Irish novelist and poet

By the 430s the Western Empire had lost too many pieces of its jigsaw of colonies to make a unified picture. To make matters worse, the nightmare was on his way.

- Attila the Hun appeared on the scene in the 440s to bring misery to the Eastern and Western Empires demanding vast sums in tributes. Like the school bully who demands the cash you had for dinner money, he was paid to go away.

- Then Marcian became emperor of the East and cut off the flow of cash to Attila. That was all the excuse the Hun needed to invade. In 451 he struck in Northern Gaul. He claimed the emperor's sister Honoria was to be his bride ... half of the Western Empire could be his dowry. Somehow the Romans under General Aetius rallied and resisted the invasion. Attila was driven back.*

- But he returned the following year – the portents must have been favourable. He was met, not by a mighty Roman army, but by Pope Leo I. Legend has it the Pope persuaded Attila to go home. The truth is Attila's army was ravaged by disease and he may have been happy to withdraw.

- Attila said he'd leave ... so long as he got his Honoria. Awwww, how sweet? Not really. He retired to his Hungarian base to await Honoria but, in need of some TLC he took another bride. On his wedding night he got drunk, had a nose-bleed and died. Or did he? One history says ...

---

* Those old soothsayers were reading sheep guts again and told Attila one of the commanders would die. This unnerved him. He turned chicken ... Attila the Hen, perhaps?

> 'Attila, King of the Huns and ravager of the provinces of
> Europe, was pierced by the hand and blade of his wife.'
>
> *Marcellinus Comes (died 534), Latin chronicler*

● OR he may have died of something like a haemor-
rhoid in his oesophagus caused by heavy drinking.
We'll never know. Did the buxom bride sing the Victorian temperance song ...?

> 'Wives, maidens and mothers, to you it is giv'n,
> To rescue the fallen and point them to heav'n.
> With us for your guides you shall win by this sign,
> The lips that touch liquor shall never touch mine.'
> *From 'The Lips that Touch Liquor Shall Never Touch Mine' (1870)*
> *by George W. Young, American lyricist*

Whatever the truth, her lips were saved ... and so was
Rome. Attila was dead. It was a respite, not a reprieve.

— FINAL CURTAINS —

> 'The end is not yet in sight, but it cannot be far away.
> The road before us is shorter than the road behind.'
> *Lucy Stone (1818–93), American abolitionist and suffragist*

Valentinian (419–455), nephew of Honorius, was a weak
and vindictive man yet he ruled for 30 years. He ruled over
the dismemberment of the Western Empire.

Predictably Valentinian killed his top general, Aetius. Murdered *personally*. In AD 454 the emperor drew his sword and attacked the unarmed general while his chamberlain joined in the butchery with (appropriately) a meat axe. As usual the excuse was that the general was getting delusions of grandeur and becoming a threat.

Yet again an emperor had removed his best commander and best hope of surviving barbarian attacks. A sort of recurring death-wish.

Bishop Sidonius Apollinaris was as baffled as we are today. He said …

> 'I am ignorant, sir, of your motives or provocations; I only know that you have acted like a man who has cut off his right hand with his left.'
>
> *Sidonius Apollinaris (430–489), Roman poet, diplomat and*
> *bishop*

Aetius had friends in low places – Hun friends – who exacted their revenge a year later. Valentinian was assassinated* while he practised archery. One Hun killed the emperor's bodyguard while the other sank a sword into the emperor's head.

Powerful plotter Petronius Maximus took the throne. He made a fatal mistake. He married off his son to Valentinian's daughter … but she'd been betrothed to Vandal leader Gaiseric's son. Furious Gaiseric sailed for Rome.

Maximus lasted just 11 weeks before Rome was panicked

---

* Vile Valentinian raped Senator Petronius Maximus's wife. The senator probably facilitated and encouraged the assassination. He certainly took over after the assassination. A bit of a clue to his involvement.

by news of the Vandal invasion. Maximus's bodyguard deserted him and a Roman mob stoned him to death as he tried to flee the city alone.

King Gaiseric marched into Rome and his Vandals sacked Rome for two weeks … vandalized it, in fact.

A Germanic soldier named Ricimer took it upon himself to be king-maker. He ruled for 14 years while his puppets were nominally on the imperial throne.

The Visigoths' second great king, Euric, unified the Visigoths and finished what Alaric had started with the famous sack on Rome in 410. In 475, the Roman government were compelled to grant the Visigoth regions of the Empire full independence. It didn't leave a lot for Rome to rule over.

Britain had expelled the representatives of Constantine III back in 410. The remaining soldiers were only bothered about keeping out the Picts and Scots to the north of Hadrian's Wall and the Angle and Saxon raiders from the east.

The Burgundians had a large chunk of France. Southern France and Spain were Visigoth territory – like Britain, a Roman province in name only. The map of Europe was a patchwork quilt of rival colours. Like the British Empire today, where in Victoria's day a quarter of the world had been coloured pink.*

The commander of the Italian forces tried to put his son, Romulus, on the throne. He was thrown off by the last of the long line of rebel generals, Odoacer.

The last? Yes, because Odoacer had the senate write to

---

* Why pink? Red was a traditional British colour but black print on red would be hard to read. Pastels made it easier, hence pink in place of red. It was 'The Empire on which the sun never sets'. It has now.

the Emperor of the East and declare ...

> 'We disclaim the necessity, or even the wish, of
> continuing the imperial succession in Italy. The
> republic may safely put its trust in the civil and
> military powers of Odoacer.'

'There is no need to have an emperor in the West.' Finis.
No emperors? No empire. Odoacer became 'administra-
tor'. The King is dead, long live the Civil Servant.*

In AD 476 the role of 'emperor' was formally abolished.
When Euric died, the Visigoths were the most powerful
state in the Western Roman Empire. The Empire in the
West was dead and within a decade a Gothic state was
established in Italy.†

BRIEF TIMELINE

AD 401 Alaric the Visigoth Christian launches an
           invasion of Italy, unopposed for a year. Stopped by
           General Stilicho the following Easter.
AD 407 When the Rhine freezes over the Vandals and
           Alans cross and invade Gaul. They won't be
           returning. Constantine III from Britain declares

---

* It didn't stop Odoacer suffering the common fate of emperors in 493.
Invited to a peace feast by Goth King Theoderic he was chopped down
by his host, who cried, 'This is what you did to my friends!' As ever,
Odoacer's innocent wife Sunigilda was killed – stoned to death – and
his brother Onoulphus was killed by archers while seeking refuge in a
church.
† The Empire in the East was more efficiently managed and survived.

himself emperor to lead the fight against the incursions into Gaul.

AD 408 The Visigoths besiege Rome for the first time but are bought off with cash and the promise that 40,000 Visigoth slaves will be freed. Stilicho's reputation is ruined by his failure to stop the barbarians and he is executed. In the Eastern Empire Theodosius II takes the throne ... aged seven.

AD 410 The Visigoths enter Rome as conquerors. They treat the citizens well and do little damage. Alaric dies as the Visigoth army marches south to invade Africa.

AD 423 When Honorius dies there are power struggles in the Western Empire. Valentinian III will end up in power.

AD 437 General Aetius struggles to hold Gaul but subdues the Franks and Bagudae outlaws. He and Valentinian can't do anything about the Vandals under Gaiseric overrunning North Africa – Rome's corn supplier.

AD 440s The Huns under Attila are masters of Gaul now. Valentinian makes Attila Military Commander of the region. But Attila has greater ambitions. He just needs an excuse to invade Italy.

AD 451 Attila the Hun invades Gaul with a vast army. The Pope meets him and persuades him to go away. Attila dies the next year but ...

AD 454 Valentinian murders top general Aetius.

AD 455 Valentinian is assassinated and the Vandals under Gaiseric sack Rome. Unlike Alaric, they do a thorough job.

AD 475 Roman General Odoacer declares there is no longer any need for an Emperor in the West. The End.

EPILOGUE

> 'I don't know why anyone but a school-boy should whine over the Empire of Rome, which grew great only by the misery of the rest of mankind. The Romans, like others, as soon as they grew rich, grew corrupt; and in their corruption sold the lives and freedoms of themselves, and of one another. A people, who while they were poor robbed mankind; and as soon as they became rich, robbed one another.'
>
> *Dr Samuel Johnson (1709–84), English writer*

The Roman Empire. What a surprise ... or two. First that it ever existed. After all, the Romans had thrown out their kings and gone out to conquer the world. What madness made them return to dictatorships? They suffered Nero and Commodus, Honorius and Elagabalus, Domitian and Caligula and still they clung on to the idea that emperors were worth the pain.

What is this human fascination with 'personality'? A hero-worship that lets evil rulers take control? Monsters like Henry VIII and Hitler, Dracula and Domitian, Mussolini and Mugabe. The list is endless. And still we don't learn from Lord Acton who warned us, 'Great men are almost always bad men.'

When an emperor let the people down they didn't say, 'Emperors are a bad idea.' They said, 'Let's replace him and hope for better luck next time.' Over and over again they deposed one with another. Madness.

> 'Insanity: doing the same thing over and over again and expecting different results.'
>
> *Albert Einstein*

Perhaps a greater surprise was that the Empire lasted for 500 years. It lasted in spite of the bad, mad, cruel and egotistical psychopaths that sat at the top of the pyramid. They made days in Rome as dangerous as any in history. Dangerous to be a Christian, then dangerous to be a pagan, dangerous to be a slave, dangerous to be an exotic animal. But most dangerous of all, being an emperor.

Greatest surprise of all? So many job applicants. Who would want that crown to their career? Would you? It increased your chances of being stabbed, strangled, poisoned, stoned or beheaded enormously. What did the job description say? 'Psychopath wanted, good pay, poor long-term prospects, would suit a sucker.'

The whining modern schoolboy was always taught that the barbarians were to blame for putting out the lights of Rome and plunging the world into the 'Dark Ages'. The truth is it was the Christians who snuffed the Roman Candle.*

---

* An ironic image since Nero set fire to the early Christians to light up his gardens at night.

> 'Blessed are the meek: for they shall inherit the earth.'
>
> *Matthew 5:5*

The meek Christian worm had turned and the meek had apparently inherited the Earth. Except the meek were armed with sharp swords and little compunction about meekly butchering those who stood in their meek way.

What would meek St Matthew have said if he'd had a crystal ball to see the horrors and the misery the followers of Christ would inflict upon the world for the next 2,000 years; non-Christians and Christians alike ... but especially fellow Christians? The Inquisition and its tortures, the witch-hunts and the burnings, the 'Holy' Wars and the Crusades.

> 'All the devastation, the butchery, the plundering, the conflagrations, and all the anguish which accompanied the recent disaster at Rome were in accordance with the general practice of warfare.'
>
> *St Augustine (354–430), 'Father of the Church'*

So that's all right then, according to Gus. It's war, lads, get over it. When in Rome (literally) do as the Romans.*

---

* Saint Augustine wasn't so saintly when it came to killing non-Christians. He created the idea of a 'Just War'. A Christian could be a soldier and serve God and country, God gave us the sword for a good reason – to protect peace and punish wickedness. Millions have died – and are still dying – following St Augustine's advice. God does indeed move in mysterious ways ...

The Christian terror inflicted on their fellow humans escalated after Alaric's sack of Rome in AD 410. And the Christians justified it.

One example of thousands ... in AD 415 the philosopher Hypatia was teaching in Alexandria and became the target of fanatical Christians led by Peter. Her crime was to suggest common sense be applied to religious beliefs. She said wise things ...

> 'To teach superstitions as truth is a most terrible thing.'
>
> *Hypatia (AD 370–415), Greek philosopher and*
> *mathematician*

Christians like the fanatical monk Cyril had no answer to that. Except violence, of course.* Hypatia was taken to a church, stripped and *'murdered with tiles'*. (One interpretation of that phrase is that her flesh was torn from her with oyster shells.) She died (of course) and her body was mutilated, her limbs burned.

In historical terms it wasn't that long (200 years) since Perpetua had been martyred for being a Christian. The wheel had turned a full circle, as the wheel of history tends to, and now Hypatia was being murdered for *not* being a Christian.†

---

* The mad monk Cyril is still revered by the Church as a saint for slicing a wicked woman apart. Jack the Ripper, who performed a similar service for humanity, is not. It's a funny old world.

† Again a woman is the victim of the dangerous days and again there is an erotic element to the violence. The Christians never gave equality to women in life, but argued that it was Eve who led Adam astray in the Garden of Eden and was responsible for sin entering the world. So women were allowed to be equal to men when it came to violent death.

The human race had a choice – experience the brutality of the Roman Empire that killed you for sport ... or the brutality of the Christian Church that killed you to save your soul.

Hobson's choice.* Ruthless rulers or vicious vicars? Maybe neither?

Ultimately the Roman Empire didn't fall because of the invaders tearing it apart. The Romans tore themselves apart. And the greatest corrosive force was greed. The ruling classes were intent on self-advancement and tried to achieve it through conspiracies and murders. The citizens of Rome allowed it so long as they had their bread and circuses – circuses steeped in blood.

> 'Crime and bad lives are the measure of a State's failure, all crime in the end is the crime of the community.'
>
> *H.G. Wells (1866–1946), English author*

The job of emperor was so very attractive the men who got there clambered over corpses to reach the top of the pile, only to add to the bloody heap themselves.

Among the corpses were the competent and the loyal, the clever administrators and the skilled generals who could have saved the Empire. Perhaps.

The Roman Republic had been thriving. Then Augustus became the first emperor. One top job. One man with the sort of power no man could handle. One title that led to all the infighting. Emperor.

---

* Thomas Hobson (1544–1631) was a livery stable owner in Cambridge. He offered customers the choice of taking the horse in the stable nearest the door or taking none at all.

Maybe Rome would have been better without an emperor. And without the Christians.

Maybe the Gallic philosopher Diderot had it right when he said …

> 'Man will never be free until the last king is strangled with the entrails of the last priest.'
>
> *Denis Diderot (1713–84), French philosopher*

The Very End

INDEX

Acte, Claudia (lover of Nero) 44
Actium, Battle of 9
Adrianople, Battle of 235–6
adultery 13, 88, 188
Aelian (Bagudae leader) 215
Aesculapius (Greek doctor) 36, 187
Agricola (Roman governor) 136
Agrippa (Roman general) 9, 12, 15
Agrippina the Elder (wife to Germanicus) 22–3
Agrippina the Younger (mother of Nero) 29, 34–5, 37–8, 40–1, 43–4, 47–8, 50–1, 53
Alamanni tribes 214
Alaric (Visigoth king) 235, 239–44, 248–50, 254
Albinus, Clodius (Roman emperor) 199–201
alectryomancy (fortune-telling) 98
Alexander of Abonutichus (Roman fortune-teller) 171–2
Alexander the Great (Macedonian king) 30
Alienus (Roman assassin) 122
Allectus (emperor of Britain and Northern Gaul) 215
Amandus (Bagudae leader) 215
Angle tribes 248

anthropomancy (fortune-telling) 97
Antinous (lover of Hadrian) 161, 165
Antonia Minor (mother of Claudius) 29
Antoninus Pius (Roman emperor) 168–71
aqueducts, ancient 12, 28
archaeologists, archaic 71, 133, 135, 148, 153, 157
Arminius (rebel leader) 58–9, 61–3, 222
armpit-hair pluckers 178
arsonists (fire-starters) 71, 75, 77–8
assassinations 7–8, 15, 27
abundant 132, 136, 145, 183, 189
asinine 37, 41, 43–5, 51–3, 84, 86
escalating 191, 200, 213, 229–30, 247, 250
astrologers, starry-eyed 95–6, 114, 146
Atlas Mountains 65
Attacotti tribes 137
Attila (Hun leader) 244–6, 250
augury (fortune-telling) 96
Augustine, Saint (Christian writer) 253

Augustus (Roman emperor) 8–19, 24–5, 39
  comparisons 123, 140, 165, 169, 255
  fortune-telling 96
  revolts against 58–9, 63–4
Aurelian (Roman emperor) 230–1, 239
Aztecs, awful 4

babies, boring 13, 15–16, 22, 27, 99, 138
bad deeds 13, 21, 29–30, 36–8, 47–50, 142–4
Bagudae (outlaws) 215, 250
baldness 31, 115, 144
barbarians 2, 4, 72
  battling 134, 162, 164, 174, 202
  boorish 229, 236, 238, 241–3, 247, 250, 252
  lowbrow 205, 214, 219–20
barrack emperors, brutal 214, 218, 230–1
Basilica 234
beauticians, blood-curdling 178
Berenice (Roman client-ruler) 122
Blandina (Christian martyr) 101
blood 24, 28, 33
  lots and clots of 44, 48, 53, 55, 67, 69–70, 88, 93, 99, 101–2, 108, 118, 130–1, 144, 169–70, 173, 182, 187, 192, 202, 206, 212–13, 218, 231, 255
boredom 26
Boudica (British queen) 47, 53, 64–74, 120
bribes 102, 113–14, 192, 197
Brigantes tribes 170
Britannia, invasion of 32–5, 39
Britannicus (son of Claudius) 35, 44, 53

brothels 36
Brutus (Roman senator) 10
Burrus, Sextus Afranius (Praetorian Guard) 43–4, 48
Byzantium 200, 236

Caesarion (son of Caesar and Cleopatra) 9–10
Caligula (Roman emperor) 24–33, 39, 41, 48, 117, 121, 138, 193, 212, 251
calm times 134–46
cannibalism 99
Caracalla (Roman emperor) 202–7, 209, 214
Caractacus (British king) 39
Carausius (emperor of Britain and Northern Gaul) 215
Cardea (door-hinge goddess) 93
Cartimandua (British queen) 39
castration, crazy 48, 114
cataclysmic times 147–58
Catherine, Saint (Christian martyr) 99
Cato the Elder (Roman writer) 169, 181
celibacy 11
Celtic tribes 223, 225–7
Ceres (cereal goddess) 2
Chaerea, Cassius (Praetorian Guard) 26–7
Chatti tribes 140–1, 223, 227
Cherusci tribes 58, 60
Christians 1–2, 45, 53
  converting 217, 232–3, 235–40, 244, 249, 252–6
  cruelty to 135, 143, 166, 170–1, 191, 199, 202, 220
  persecution 83, 89–92, 100, 105, 109–10, 123, 214
Cicero (Roman orator) 68
circumcision 168, 211

Circus Maximus 76–8, 81
circuses, crazed 12, 76–8, 81, 96, 195, 255
Claudius II (Roman emperor) 214
Claudius (Roman emperor) 24–5, 27, 29, 33–42, 53, 96, 141, 193
Cleander (freedman of Commodus) 188–90
Cleopatra (Egyptian queen) 9–10, 122
Cloaca Maxima (Roman sewer) 12
Cloacina (sewer goddess) 12
cobwebs, collecting 211
Coliseum 1, 118–19, 123, 135, 141, 143
Columella (Roman cookery writer) 181
Commodus (Roman emperor) 134, 170–1, 174, 184–92, 196, 200, 202, 251
Constantine III (Roman client-king) 248–9
Constantine (Roman emperor) 92, 105, 108, 110–11, 232–3, 235–6
Constantinople 234, 236, 243
Constantius II (Roman emperor) 236
coprolites (fossilized faeces) 152
Corbulo, Domitius (Roman military leader) 43, 47
cramps 40
criminals 26, 28, 96, 141, 185, 193
crises 208–18
Crispina, Bruttia (wife to Commodus) 188
Criton (doctor of Trajan) 228
crucifixions 59, 71, 83
    crowd-pulling 127, 129, 220, 236
    excruciating 89, 91, 106–9, 123
currency, devalued 46, 212, 219

curses 24, 66, 100, 147, 153, 205

Dacian (Roman emperor) 102–3, 105–6
Dacian tribes 136, 160–2, 227–9, 239
Danube, River 162, 170, 216, 228, 235, 239
decapitations 37, 71
Decebalus (Roman client-king) 135, 137, 160–2, 228–9
Decianus, Catus (Roman financial agent) 68, 71
Decius (Roman emperor) 216
decline and fall 230–50
diarrhoea 40, 119
Didymus, Arius (Roman teacher) 10
Dio, Cassius (Roman historian) 67, 71, 76, 140–1, 174, 185, 211
Diocletian (Roman emperor) 103–6, 215, 232
disastrous times 75–90
disembowelling 67, 209
Disraeli, Benjamin (British prime minister) 43, 45, 175
divination (fortune-telling) 94–8, 222
Domitian (Roman emperor) 124, 130, 134, 134–46, 159, 162, 193, 229, 251
Doryphoros (lover of Nero) 44–5
drooling 25, 27, 35
Druids 65–7, 227
Drusilla (sister of Caligula) 32
Drusus (stepson of Augustus) 15
Drusus (stepson of Tiberius) 23
dry cleaners 179

earthquakes 100, 148–9
Eastern Empire 105, 121, 235–6, 243–5, 249–50

economic problems 20, 160, 213, 215, 219

Elagabal (sun god) 209

Elagabalus (Roman emperor) 181, 202, 208–12, 251

elephants 39

enemas, execrable 41

Ennius (Roman cynic) 95–6

entrails, interesting 67, 93, 149, 256

Epaphroditus (secretary of Domitian) 145

Epidosus (Christian martyr) 101

Eulalia (Christian martyr) 106

Eunia (wife to Macro) 29

eunuchs, useless 27, 41, 122, 138, 211

Euric (Visigoth king) 248–9

Eusebius (Roman historian) 104

executions 4, 10–11, 19
endless 23, 27, 29, 31–4, 37–9, 43, 45, 47, 49, 53–4, 57, 84, 86, 89, 100–2, 104–9, 113, 116, 118, 122, 130, 139, 144–5, 148, 164, 185, 188–9, 191–2, 197, 204, 206–7, 209–11, 225, 231, 234, 241

extispicy (fortune-telling) 96

Facebook 154

famine 31, 99–100

fast-food vendors 180

feudal system 225

flaying (skinning alive) 218

floggings 38, 45, 68–9, 108

Florus, Gessius (Roman governor) 126–7

food 180–3, 221, 235, 242

Fox, Peter (British doctor) 5–6, 42, 107–8, 130–1, 152, 173, 218

Frankish tribes 214–15, 236–7, 250

fratricide (sibling-killing) 188–9, 206

French Revolution 4

Furrina (miscellaneous goddess) 94

Gaetulicus (German governor) 33

Gaiseric (Vandal king) 247–8, 250

Gaius (grandson of Augustus) 15–16

Galba (Roman emperor) 112–14, 116–18, 128, 135

Galban (Roman governor) 54

Galen (Turkish physician) 184, 187

Galerian (Roman emperor) 105, 109

Gallic tribes 223–5

Gallienus (Roman emperor) 105, 217

Gemellus (cousin of Caligula) 29, 32

genocide (whole-group-killing) 223, 227

Germanic tribes 220–3, 228

Germanicus (father of Caligula) 18, 22, 25–6

Geta (son of Septimius Severus) 202–3, 205–6

gibbets, gory 107

Gibbon, Edward (British historian) 134–5, 167, 174, 190

Giora, Simon Bar (Jewish rebel) 125–6, 130

gladiators 3, 12, 29–30
glorious 55, 123, 135, 141–3, 146
gorgeous 185, 187, 190–5, 212

gods 8, 32, 40
emperors as 2, 11, 25, 31, 33–4, 54, 119, 138, 146, 186, 203

grotesque 149, 158, 171–2, 187, 192, 209, 214, 227, 234, 237
old 12, 62, 92–5, 98, 102, 105–6, 110, 116, 126, 143
gold 26, 32, 54–5
grasping for 191, 217, 227–9, 243
greed for 82, 114, 116, 123, 130, 143, 162, 174
good deeds 12, 20, 28, 35–6, 46–7, 140–2
Goth tribes 214, 216, 235–6, 239–40, 249
graffiti 153–4
Graves, Robert (English writer) 34
Great Fire of Rome 48, 53, 75–84, 89, 99
Greek tragedies 90
Guillotin, Dr (French inventor) 4
guts 63, 96–8, 180, 187, 209, 245

Hadrian (Roman emperor) 137, 160–1, 163–8, 170
Hadrian's Wall 137, 164–7, 169–70, 248
hairdressers 177
hangovers 8
haruspicy (fortune-telling) 96–7
hemlock (poisonous plant) 88
Herculaneum 148–9, 152, 155–6
Herod Agrippa II (Roman client-king) 122
Herod (Roman client-king) 15, 132
Hilarian (Roman governor) 2–3
Hilarius (Roman emperor) 104
Homer (Greek poet) 103
Honoria (sister of Marcian) 245
Honorius (Roman emperor) 241–4, 246, 250–1
hooliganism 194

horse armour 222
humorism 187
Hun tribes 235–6, 239, 244–7, 250
hurricanes 89
Hypatia (Greek philosopher) 254

Iceni tribes 64–74
impalings, improper 71, 212
incest, incredible 38, 47, 99, 122
Incitatus (horse of Caligula) 30
Industrial Revolution 175
insurrections 120–33
Isis (Egyptian goddess) 83, 96

jaundice 40
Jerome, Saint (Christian writer) 137, 243
Jesus 15, 23, 91, 104, 107–8, 110, 190
Jewish tribes 15, 59, 83
rebelling 120–33, 135, 163, 167–8, 170
resisting 89–92, 98–9, 109, 117
John of Giscala (Jewish rebel) 125–6
John, Saint (Christian apostle) 91
Josephus (Jewish historian) 129, 132
Julia (daughter of Augustus) 15
Julia the Elder (wife to Augustus) 18
Julia (grand-daughter of Augustus) 13
Julia (niece of Claudius) 38
Julianus, Didius (Roman emperor) 198–9
Julius Caesar (Roman geezer) 7–8, 10–11, 34, 39, 64, 118, 183, 223–5
Juvenal (Roman poet) 142, 183, 195

Kokhba, Simon Bar (Jewish rebel) 169–70

labyrinths, long 97
Laetus (Roman general) 197–8
Latin language 82–3, 95, 108, 126, 215, 238
leeches, slimy 177
lemmings, leaping 103–4
Leo I (Christian pope) 245
Lepidus, Marcus (brother-in-law of Caligula) 29
lice, lousy 177
Licinius (Roman emperor) 236
lictors (Roman floggers) 69
limes 165–6
Livia (mother of Tiberius) 16–17
Livilla (wife to Drusus) 23
loans 70
Locusta (Roman poisoner) 41, 44, 55
lottery tickets 211
Lucilla (sister of Commodus) 188–9, 191–2
Lucius (grandson of Augustus) 15
Lucius (Roman co-emperor) 169–70, 172–3
lucky charms 95
Lugdunum, Battle of 201

Machiavelli, Niccolò (Italian philosopher) 196–7
Macrinus (Roman emperor) 207, 209
Macro (best friend of Caligula) 29
mad deeds 14–15, 22, 30–1, 38, 50–2, 144–5
Maesa, Julia (grandmother of Elagabalus) 209, 211–12
Marcia (mistress of Commodus) 191–2
Marcian (Roman emperor) 245

Marcomanni tribes 171
Marcus Aurelius (Roman emperor) 101, 105, 135, 169–74, 187
Mark Antony (Roman dictator) 8–10, 122
Martial (Roman historian) 195
Martialis, Julius (bodyguard of Caracalla) 207
martyrs, many 2, 23, 45, 83, 91–2, 98–110, 134, 217, 254
massacres, merciless 71–2, 74, 127, 136, 140, 169, 171, 206, 238
Matthew, Saint (Christian apostle) 232, 237, 253
Maturus (Christian martyr) 101–2
Maxentius (Roman emperor) 99, 234
Maximian (Roman emperor) 182, 215
Maximus, Petronius (Roman emperor) 247–8
mazes, amazing 97
measles 170, 172–3
megalomania, madness of 45, 53
Messalina (wife to Claudius) 25, 33–4, 36–7, 39
military anarchy 212–18
mines, not yours 39, 162, 229
mobs, angry 12, 24, 55, 101–2, 116, 171, 189–90, 206, 239, 248
morals 4, 13, 45, 102, 138–9, 158, 238
mushrooms, dodgy 40–2

Naissus, Battle of 214
Nemesis 219–29
nepotism (family-favouritism) 59
Nero (Roman emperor) 37–8, 40, 43–57

comparisons 138, 146–7, 174,
184, 194, 196, 212
Great Fire 76–88, 90
instability 112, 114, 116
insurrections 120–1, 127, 251
persecution 70, 74, 92, 99–100,
105, 252
Nerva (Roman emperor) 136,
159–60
Niger, Pescennius (Roman
emperor) 199–201
Nile, River 46, 165
Numerian (Roman emperor) 231

Octavia (wife to Nero) 40, 44, 48,
53
Octavian see Augustus
Odoacer (rebel general) 248–50
Olympic Games 49, 90, 192
omens, occult 96, 114, 147, 222
oracles, consulting 216, 222
orgies, ogling at 15
Orwell, George (British novelist)
206
Otho (Roman emperor) 112–16,
128, 135, 145

pagans 2, 235, 252
Paris (Roman actor) 49, 144
Parthenius (chamberlain of
Domitian) 145–6
Parthian tribes 43, 47, 171, 214
parties, wild 8, 84, 145, 182
Paul, Saint (Christian missionary)
53, 89, 111
Paulinus, Gaius Suetonius
(Roman general) 47, 65–7, 71,
73–4
pax Romana 135, 167
Penates (cupboard gods) 93
Perpetua, Vibia (Christian
martyr) 1–6, 104, 199, 254

persecution, pesky 89, 91–111,
214, 217, 232, 236, 240
Persian tribes 216–17, 235–6
Pertinax (Roman emperor)
197–8, 201
Peter, Saint (Christian apostle)
89, 254
Petro, Titus Flavius (great-
grandfather of Titus) 121
Petronius (Roman writer) 48
Pharsalus, Battle of 121
Philip the Arab (Roman emperor)
216
Pictish tribes 205, 236, 248
Pilate, Pontius (Roman governor)
23
pimples 21
Pionius (Christian martyr) 103
pirates 215
Piso, Gaius (Roman senator)
52–3, 84–5, 87
plagues 89, 135, 147, 170, 172–4,
187–8, 213, 219
Plautianus (Praetorian Guard)
203
plebs 141, 177–81, 190, 211
Pliny the Elder (Roman writer)
20, 150–2
Pliny the Younger (Roman writer)
100, 150, 153, 157
Plotina (wife to Trajan) 161, 163
Plutarch (Roman historian)
223–4
poison 7, 22–3, 25
plentiful 74, 119, 138, 152
polluting 156, 178, 187, 192,
211, 238
putrid 29, 38, 40–2, 44–5, 50, 55,
63
Polla, Acerronia (companion of
Agrippina) 51
Pompeii 135, 148–51, 154–8, 194

Pompey, Gaius (son-in-law of Claudius) 38
Pompey (Roman dictator) 121
Ponticus (Christian martyr) 101
poo, paddling in 12
Poppaea (wife to Nero) 44–5, 48, 53, 114, 178
posh people 12, 179, 181
Postumus (Roman emperor) 214, 217, 225
Pothinus, Bishop (Christian martyr) 101
pottery, precious 59, 133, 228
Praetorian Guard 19, 22, 26–8
  powerful 81, 87, 113–14, 116, 160
  prevalent 191, 197–9, 203–4, 207, 211
  priceless 33, 37, 39, 43–5, 48, 54–5
Prasutagus (British client-king) 67–8, 70
Probus (Roman emperor) 231
prostitution 30, 124, 210
psychopaths 252
Ptolemy (Roman client-king) 33
puppet rulers 67, 171, 233, 248
purges 92, 136, 144, 206
pus 173
pyroclastic surges 149, 155–7
pyromaniacs 80
Pythagoras (marriage partner to Nero) 49

rape 23, 68, 70, 171, 234, 247
rebels 58–74
revolting times 58–74
Rhine, River 140, 214, 242, 249
Rhone, River 201
roads 39, 228

Robigus (mildew god) 93
Romulus (Italian leader) 248

Sabazius (beer god) 93
Sabina (wife to Hadrian) 161
Sabinus (Roma governor) 136
sacrifices 62, 66–7, 92–3
  scary 96, 100, 102–3, 105–6, 115, 126–7
  shedloads of 130, 149, 192, 209, 214, 227
Salvian (Christian writer) 220
Saturninus (Roman governor) 136, 143–4
Saxon tribes 248
Scaevinus, Flavius (Roman property owner) 85–7
scandals 21, 138, 209
scatomancy (fortune-telling) 97
Segestes (father-in-law of Arminius) 61
Sejanus (Roman general) 19–20, 22–3, 29
Seneca the Younger (Roman historian) 40, 43–5, 48, 54–6, 87–9, 201
Severianus (Roman governor) 171
Severus, Alexander (Roman emperor) 213
Severus, Septimius (Roman emperor) 2, 198–205
sewers 12, 156, 212
sex, sloppy 11, 21, 28, 36, 41, 99, 112–13, 138
shadow emperors 232–3
shameful times 184–95
Siculus, Diodorus (Greek writer) 226
Silanus, Marcus Junius (father-in-law of Caligula) 29, 37
sin 254

skinning 217–18

skulls 21, 63, 124, 143, 150

slaves 14, 21, 29–30
    shiftless 81, 88, 102–3, 107, 123, 132
    slogging 211, 223–4, 227–9, 235, 243, 250, 252
    suffering 36, 39, 43–4, 49, 63, 73
    sundry 151, 163, 181, 189, 192, 194, 197

small print, invented 27

smallpox 170, 172

smothering 24–5

snot 173

soothsayers (fortune-tellers) 30–1, 245

Spartacus (rebel leader) 107

Spiculus (gladiator of Nero) 55

spies 19

spit 118, 173

spivs 195

splanchomancy (fortune-telling) 97

Sporus/Sabina (marriage partner to Nero) 48, 114

stabbings, several 3, 7, 27, 38, 45, 54, 86, 115, 122, 139, 146, 185, 189, 211

stable times 159–74

stammering 25, 27

starvation 23, 29, 38
    incessant 183, 189, 211, 218
    relentless 41, 116, 129, 149, 165

Statilia Messalina (wife to Nero) 49

Stilicho (Roman general) 232 240–2, 249–50

Stoics 170

Strabo (Greek writer) 226

strangulation 23, 85, 107, 192, 204, 225, 227, 256

Suetonius (Roman historian) 14, 24–5, 40, 47, 76, 112, 115, 124, 140, 146, 151

suffocation 48, 88, 152, 156–7, 227, 234

suicide (self-killing) 22–3, 29, 45, 48, 51, 87, 89, 104, 117, 133, 171, 196, 219

Sun Bin (Chinese military strategist) 9, 60–1

Sun Tzu (Chinese military strategist) 9

superstitions, silly 221–2, 254

Tacitus (Roman historian) 19, 60, 66–7, 70–1, 73, 76–7, 84, 113, 136, 141, 222–3

Tarpeian Rock, throwing people from 130–1, 133, 162

Tarquinius Superbus, Lucius (Roman king) 7

tasseography (tea-leaf reading) 96

taxes, terrible 27, 30, 53, 82, 113, 119, 160, 190, 202, 211, 215

teachers, tiresome 10, 43, 54, 56, 60, 87–8, 138, 144, 196

Terminus (boundary-marker god) 93

Tetrarchy 232

Thames, River 70, 72

Theodosius II (Roman emperor) 250

Theodosius (Roman emperor) 236, 240, 244

Third Reich 58

Tiber, River 12, 23, 55, 172, 212, 234

Tiberius (Roman emperor) 13, 16–25, 28–9, 32, 41, 116, 133

Tigellinus (Praetorian Guard) 45, 48

timelines, tedious 15–16, 22–3, 32–3, 39–40, 53–4, 105, 135–7, 160, 170, 202, 214–15, 236–7, 249–50
Titus (Roman emperor) 119, 121–30, 132, 135, 138, 147–8, 157
toilets 21, 94, 119, 179, 183, 211
torture 15, 23, 29
   interminable 31, 38, 83, 85, 87, 101–2, 104, 106, 116
   tormenting 125, 136, 171, 229, 244, 253
tourism 148, 157, 204
Trajan (Roman emperor) 100, 105, 123, 136, 159–63, 228–9
treason 11, 26, 47–8, 53, 145
treasury 29, 118
trespassing 93, 107
trousers, banned 241
Tullia (wife to Tarquinius Superbus) 7
turmoil 196–202

Unconquered Sun (religion) 110–11
unstable times 112–19
urine, unpleasant 119, 177, 179
uromancy (fortune-telling) 97
uxoricide (wife-killing) 188

Valens (Roman emperor) 98, 235–6
Valentinian (Roman emperor) 246–7, 250
Valerian (Roman emperor) 105, 214, 217
Vandal tribes 247–50
Varus, Publius Quinctilius

(Roman general) 14, 59, 61–4
Vercingetorix (rebel leader) 224–5
Verica (British king) 39
Vespasian (Roman emperor) 116–19, 121–2, 127–9, 135–6
Vesta (pagan goddess) 11
Vestal Virgins (Roman priestesses) 9, 11–12, 138–9, 209
Vesuvius, Mount 135, 147–58
Victorians, vile 4, 175, 246, 248
Virgil (Roman poet) 84, 94
Visigoth tribes 235, 239–40, 250
Vitellius (Roman emperor) 112–13, 115–18, 128, 135, 143–4
volcanic eruptions 135, 147–58
Vologases (Parthian rebel) 171
vomit 183, 192, 218
voyeurism, vulgar 21, 138
Vulcan (fire god) 149

war, just 253
Weser, River 60
Western Empire 105, 109, 215, 234, 240–1, 244–6, 249–50
whoopee cushions 210
wicker cages, burnings in 62
wigs, wearing 115
wind, breaking 36, 210
woad (blue body dye) 64, 227

Xenophon (doctor of Claudius) 41

Year of 4 Emperors 112, 117, 119, 135, 196
Year of 5 Emperors 196–7, 202
Year of 6 Emperors 202, 213

Zealots (Jewish rebels) 132–3